DELEUZE AND GUATTARI'S
ANTI-OEDIPUS

Continuum *Reader's Guides*

Continuum's *Reader's Guides* are clear, concise and accessible introductions to classic works of philosophy. Each book explores the major themes, historical and philosophical context and key passages of a major philosophical text, guiding the reader toward a thorough understanding of often demanding material. Ideal for undergraduate students, the guides provide an essential resource for anyone who needs to get to grips with a philosophical text.

Reader's Guides available from Continuum

DELEUZE AND GUATTARI'S
ANTI-OEDIPUS
A Reader's Guide

IAN BUCHANAN

continuum

Continuum International Publishing Group
The Tower Building   80 Maiden Lane
11 York Road   Suite 704
London SE1 7NX   New York, NY 10038
www.continuumbooks.com

First published 2008

British Library Cataloguing-in-Publication Data
A catalogue record for this book is available from the British Library.

ISBN-10: PB: 0-8264-9149-9

ISBN-13: PB: 978-0-8264-9149-7

Library of Congress Cataloging-in-Publication Data
Buchanan, Ian, 1969–
Deleuze and Guattari's Anti-Oedipus: a reader's guide / Ian Buchanan.
        p. cm.
Includes bibliographical references (p.) and index.
ISBN 978-0-8264-9149-7 1. Deleuze, Gilles,
    1925–1995. 2. Guattari, Félix, 1930–1992. 3. Deleuze, Gilles,
1925–1995. Anti-Œdipe. 4. Social psychiatry. 5. Schizophrenia–Social
    aspects. 6. Capitalism–Social aspects. I. Title.
                 RC455.B83   2008
                 362.2'6—dc22
                                            2007023443

Typeset by Servis Filmsetting Ltd, Manchester
Printed and bound in Great Britain by MPG Books Ltd,
Bodmin, Cornwall

For Bent Meier Sørensen

CONTENTS

ACKNOWLEDGEMENTS

I would particularly like to thank Hanjo Berressem and all the students who attended the 'Got no pappamummy' workshop on whom I tried out a number of the ideas this book develops. I must thank, too, Claire Colebrook, William Connolly, Sarah Campbell (my very patient editor), Martin Fuglsang, Fredric Jameson, Christian Kerslake, Gregg Lambert, John Marks, Negar Mottahedeh, Paul Patton, Adrian Parr, Patricia Pisters, David Rodowick, Marc Rölli, Horst Ruthrof, David Savat, Daniel W. Smith, Bent Meier Sørensen, Marcel Swiboda, Nick Thoburn and James Williams – each, in their own way, stimulated me to see Deleuze and Guattari's work differently. None can be blamed for *how* differently I've seen things.

Again, I must thank Tanya Buchanan . . . *we've gone a long way baby, you and I.*

Special thanks, too, to Courtney and Sebastian who mostly kept the noise down, mostly.

Cardiff, May 2007

A NOTE ON THE TEXT

This book is a sequel to *Deleuzism*. It provides more detail on the connection between Deleuze's work and dialectics, a connection that I'm no longer the only one to see. But it also tries something different, which I call 'practical Deleuzism'.

ABBREVIATIONS

Page references given within the text are first to the English translation and second the original French. It should be noted that the new
Continuum editions of Deleuze and Guattari's works are differently
paginated to the previous Athlone and University of Minnesota
Press editions.

Works by Deleuze and Guattari

(AO) Deleuze, G. and Guattari, F. (2004) [new edition]
Anti-Oedipus, translated by Robert Hurley, Mark Seem and Helen
R Lane, London and New York: Continuum.
  Deleuze, G. and Guattari, F. (2002) [nouvelle édition augmentée]
L'Anti-Oedipe: Capitalisme et Schizophrénie, Paris: Éditions de Minuit.
(ATP) Deleuze, G. and Guattari, F. (2004) [new edition] *A
Thousand Plateaus*, translated by Brian Massumi, London and New
York: Continuum.
  Deleuze, G. and Guattari, F. (2001) *Mille Plateaux: Capitalisme
et Schizophrénie 2*, Paris: Éditions de Minuit.
(WiP?) Deleuze, G. and Guattari, F. (1994) *What is Philosophy?*,
translated by Hugh Tomlinson and Graham Burchell, New York:
Columbia University Press.
  Deleuze, G. and Guattari, F. (1991) *Qu'est-ce que la philosophie?*,
Paris: Éditions de Minuit.
(K) Deleuze, G. and Guattari, F. (1986) *Kafka: Toward a Minor
Literature*, translated by Dana Polan, Minneapolis: University of
Minnesota Press.
  Deleuze, G. and Guattari, F. (2005) *Kafka: Pour une Littérature
Mineure*, Paris: Éditions de Minuit.

Works by Deleuze

(TRM)   Deleuze, G. (2006) *Two Regimes of Madness: Texts and Interviews 1975–1995*, edited by David Lapoujade, New York: Semiotext(e).

Deleuze, G. (2003) *Deux Régimes de Fous: Textes et Entretiens 1975–1995*, Paris: Éditions de Minuit.

(C1)   Deleuze, G. (2005) *Cinema 1: The Movement-Image*, translated by Hugh Tomlinson and Robert Galeta, London: Continuum.

Deleuze, G. (1983) *Cinéma 1: L'image-mouvement*, Paris: Éditions de Minuit.

(C2)   Deleuze, G. (2005) *Cinema 2: The Time-Image*, translated by Hugh Tomlinson and Robert Galeta, London: Contiuum.

Deleuze, G. (1985) *Cinéma 2: L'image-temps*, Paris: Éditions de Minuit.

(DI)   Deleuze, G. (2004) *Desert Islands and Other Texts 1953–1974*, edited by David Lapoujade, New York: Semiotext(e).

Deleuze, G. (2002) *L'île Déserte et Autres Textes: Textes et Entretiens 1953–1974*, Paris: Éditions de Minuit.

(PS)   Deleuze, G. (2000) *Proust and Signs: The Complete Text*, translated by R. Howard, Minneapolis: University of Minnesota Press.

(CC)   Deleuze, G. (1997) *Essays Critical and Clinical*, translated by Daniel W. Smith and Michael A. Greco, Minneapolis: University of Minnesota Press.

(N)   Deleuze, G. (1995) *Negotiations*, translated by Martin Joughin, New York: Columbia University Press.

Deleuze, G. (2003) *Pourparlers 1972–1990*, Paris: Éditions de Minuit.

(DR)   Deleuze, G. (1994) *Difference and Repetition*, translated by Paul Patton, London: Athlone.

Deleuze, G. (2005) *Différence et repetition*, Paris: Presses Universitaires de France.

(ES)   Deleuze, G. (1991) *Empiricism and Subjectivity: An Essay on Hume's Theory of Human Nature*, translated by Constantin Boundas, New York: Columbia University Press.

Deleuze, G. (1998) [sixth edition] *Empirisme et Subjectivité: Essai sur la Nature Humaine selon Hume*, Paris: Presses Universitaires de France.

(D)   Deleuze, G. and Parnet, C. (1987) [new edition] *Dialogues II*, translated by Hugh Tomlinson and Barbara Habberjam, London: Continuum.

Deleuze, G. and Parnet, C. (1996) *Dialogues*, Paris: Flammarion.

(NP) Deleuze, G. (1983) *Nietzche and Philosophy*, translated by Hugh Tomlinson, London: Athlone.

Deleuze, G. (2003) [fourth edition] *Nietzsche et la philosophie*, Paris: Presses Universitaires de France.

Works by Guattari

(AOP) Guattari, F. (2006) *The Anti-Oedipus Papers*, edited by Stéphane Nadaud, translated by Kélina Gotman, New York: Semiotext(e).

Guattari, F. (2004) *Écrits pour L'Anti-Oedipe*, edited by Stéphane Nadaud, Paris: Lignes-Manifeste.

(CY) Guattari, F. (1995) *Chaosophy*, edited by Sylvère Lotringer, New York: Semiotext(e).

CHAPTER 1

DELEUZE AND GUATTARI IN CONTEXT

We were only two, but what was important for us was less our working together than this strange fact of working between the two of us. We stopped being 'author'.

Gilles Deleuze and Claire Parnet, *Dialogues*

Naively I thought 'together' must mean 'with my friends, the gang'. But that didn't last long! I quickly understood that it would only be the two of us. It was a frenzy of work that I hadn't imagined possible until then.

Félix Guattari, *Chaosophy*

In the always exacting judgement of Perry Anderson, Louis Athusser's near hegemonic sway over Western Marxism and indeed critical theory in general throughout the 1960s declined absolutely in the aftermath of May '68 because his thought did not provide a coherent response to what happened that summer.[1] Even if he did not approve of the turn their work took, Anderson would probably agree to the related proposition that Deleuze and Guattari burst into the limelight in the same period precisely because *their work did* provide a coherent response to the Events of May. This does not mean, however, that we need accept Anderson's description of what he calls 'the moment of *Anti-Oedipus*' as the irruption of 'saturnalian subjectivism'.[2] The resulting work is both more complex and dare I say less irrational than Anderson allows. That being said, Anderson's verdict on the state of Western Marxism as a whole in this period does apply to Deleuze and Guattari's work and may serve here to put their project into perspective in a very immediate fashion. Anderson's greatest disappointment – if that is the right word, and

I'm not sure it is – concerning the development of theory in the 1960s and 1970s was its failure in the area he referred to as 'strategy', 'that is, any elaboration of a concrete or plausible perspective for a transition beyond capitalist democracy to a socialist democracy'.[3] What has to be remembered here, however, is that although this indictment is framed in such a way that it seems to take aim at individual theorists, and clearly Anderson wants to call theorists like Deleuze and Guattari to account, it actually applies to the situation itself. As Fredric Jameson put it, refuting criticisms of Theodor Adorno's alleged break with Marxism: 'It is not, indeed, people who change, but rather situations.'[4]

The perceived failure of the Events of May (a viewpoint Deleuze and Guattari did not subscribe to) led to a situation for which Alain Badiou has supplied the apt concept of 'Thermidorean' to describe: it was a moment in which strategic thinking was rendered unthinkable.[5] Thus the challenge of Western Marxism in the aftermath of May '68 was not to supply the strategy to go with the theory, as Anderson demands, but to use theory to cleanse strategy of its fatal taint of impracticality. This is the challenge *Anti-Oedipus* answers and it does so by providing a genealogy of desire, showing how and when it came to be enchained. It is true that in the closing pages of *Anti-Oedipus* Deleuze and Guattari quite explicitly state that their work does not offer a model to follow; but then again, their thesis in a nutshell is that if we understand desire properly and distinguish it effectively from interest then the revolution *is already* made. This revolution is, however, in constant danger of being permanently postponed: witness Nicholas Sarkozy's ominous proclamation in the lead up to the 2007 French presidential election: 'We have two days to liquidate the legacy of May 1968!'[6]

WHEN GILLES MET FÉLIX

Gilles Deleuze and Félix Guattari met in the summer of 1969. Deleuze says of their meeting that Guattari was the one who sought him out, that at the time he didn't even know who he was. Evidently their meeting went well because Deleuze suggested they work together.[7] A lot of ink has been spilled speculating about how their collaboration worked in practice, all too often with the nefarious motive of sorting out who wrote what. It seems to me, however, that Deleuze says it all when he says that they each thought that the other had gone further than they had and therefore they could learn from each other. In conversation with Claire Parnet, Deleuze described his way of working with Guattari as a 'pick-up' method, but then qualifies it by saying 'method' is not the right word and suggests 'double-theft' and 'a-parallel evolution' as perhaps better alternatives (D, 18/25).

> It started off with letters. And then we began to meet from time to time to listen to what the other had to say. It was great fun. But it could be really tedious too. One of us always talked too much. Often one of us would put forward some notion, and the other just didn't see it, wouldn't be able to make anything of it until months later, in a different context. [. . .] And then we wrote a lot. Félix sees writing as a schizoid flow drawing in all sorts of things. I'm interested in the way a page of writing flies off in all directions and at the same time closes right up on itself like an egg. And in the reticences, the resonances, the lurches, and all the larvae you can find in a book. Then we really started writing together, it wasn't a problem. We took turns at rewriting things. (N, 14/25)

In 1969 Gilles Deleuze was 44 and having just completed his Doctorat D'Etat he was the very epitome of a respectable professor. This was indeed how even his friends regarded him. 'Deleuze was a delightful character,' Antonio Negri would say later, 'but he was a professor, an intellectual!'[8] Similarly, Guattari informs us that he had hoped his collaboration with Deleuze would mean that Deleuze would get out more and get more involved in political action, yet it seemed to have the opposite effect (CY, 28).[9] This should not be taken to mean that Deleuze was inactive or uninvolved politically.[10] It simply acknowledges that his preference was to conduct politics through his writing by promulgating new forms of thought via the invention of new concepts. Deleuze more or less affirms this himself when he declares that one shouldn't travel around too much because it interferes with one's becoming (N, 138/188). Yet in spite of his aloofness, this extremely scholarly professor clearly exerted a powerful intellectual magnetism in his seminars and in his books.

Viewers of *L'Abécédaire de Gilles Deleuze*, a remarkable eight-hour dialogue (Deleuze explicitly refused to do an interview) between Deleuze and Claire Parnet recorded for French television in 1988, but only screened after his death, can see this clearly.[11] Prefacing the interview there is a tantalizingly brief glimpse, in grainy, poorly lit black and white footage, of one of Deleuze's seminars at the University of Vincennes in 1980, which shows a relatively small room filled to capacity with evidently spellbound students.[12] The plain, functional table at which Deleuze is seated is covered with an array of tape recorders and microphones, the desiring-machines of a new generation of students. Richard Pinhas, experimental musician and dedicated Deleuzian, was one of those new kinds of students with a tape recorder. He made recordings of dozens of Deleuze's seminars, which he has now made available on the web at webdeleuze.com. In the process he has inaugurated an incredible, spontaneous collective archival project aimed at making Deleuze's teaching as accessible as possible: the recordings have been transcribed and translated into several languages, thus providing Deleuze scholars with an invaluable resource.[13]

Intellectually Deleuze defined himself against the generation that came before him – he respected and admired his teachers, but nonetheless rejected their teaching very firmly. 'I could not stand Descartes, the dualisms and the Cogito, or Hegel, the triad and the operation of the negation.' (D, 14/21). The one exception was Sartre.[14] In his early student days, he saw Sartre as a breath of fresh air, but did not feel drawn to existentialism or phenomenology (D, 12/18). Novelist Michel Tournier recalled that even then as an undergraduate Deleuze was already a powerful innovator:

> We soon came to fear his talent for seizing upon a single one of our words and using it to expose our banality, stupidity, or failure of intelligence. He possessed extraordinary powers of translation and rearrangement: all the tired philosophy of the curriculum passed through him and emerged unrecognisable but rejuvenated, with a fresh, undigested, bitter taste of newness that we weaker, lazier minds found disconcerting and repulsive.[15]

In his own description of his student days, Deleuze said he belonged to a generation, 'that was more or less bludgeoned to death with the history of philosophy' (N, 5/14). What Deleuze objected to was the repressive way this history of philosophy was used to wrap thought in the straightjacket of the imperative injunction 'you can't do this until you've read that', which all students are familiar with.

Deleuze's way of escaping this was to think of 'the history of philosophy as a sort of buggery or (it comes to the same thing) immaculate conception. I saw myself as taking an author from behind and giving him a child that would be his own offspring, yet monstrous.' (N, 6/15). His monographs on Hume, Bergson, Nietzsche and Spinoza, written in the early part of his career, do not put words into the mouths of their subjects, but are nonetheless able to make them say something quite different to the received view of them. But more importantly, these books enabled Deleuze to think differently; they were his lines of flight, or 'witch's brooms' (D, 15/22), that took him outside and beyond the confines of his situation, giving him the freedom to do philosophy for himself. By his own estimation, he did not really begin to do philosophy for himself until he wrote *Différence and Répétition*, the major thesis for his Doctorat D'Etat. It was this book, according to Deleuze, particularly chapter 3 'The Image of Thought', which concerns precisely the conditions of possibility for producing radically new thought, that paved the way to his collaborative work with Guattari (D, xvii).

A few years younger than Deleuze, Félix Guattari was only 37 in 1969. At this point in his career he had neither a degree nor a book to his name. Again, Negri provides a vivid portrait highlighting the contrasting personalities of the two future collaborators. Speaking of Deleuze, Negri says: 'We talked about many things, but I couldn't tell him that I was depressed, that I was tired, that I had problems. I couldn't ask him to do anything for me. It was difficult to explain to him what was happening in Italy. With Félix I could. Very soon we began to come up with ideas together – and not only from the theoretical point of view.'[16] Guattari had a gift for organizing people, for bringing them together and engineering a creative spark between them. It was almost as if he was the living embodiment of 'transversality', the concept he invented to describe relations between subjects and objects, or subjects and subjects, which is neither unifying nor totalizing. Before he met Deleuze, Guattari had already gained notoriety in France as a political activist. He was known in the French press as 'Mr Anti-' for his public campaigning on a range of causes from the decolonization of Algeria, the improved treatment of prisoners in French prisons (he was a member of Michel Foucault's Groupe d'Information sur les Prisons), the improved treatment of the mentally ill in French insane asylums, the establishment of free radio, to Gay rights and Green politics. In 1973 he outraged national sensibilities by publishing a special issue of the journal *Recherches* edited by Guy Hocquenghem and René Schérer provocatively entitled 'Three Billion Perverts: An Encyclopaedia of Homosexualities'.[17] French courts banned it and ordered all copies destroyed. Guattari was also fined, but he proudly never paid. More controversially, he collaborated with Negri, who was arrested in 1977 on charges of terrorism for his association with the Red Brigades. Guattari also spoke against the extradition from Germany to France of Klaus Croissant, a German lawyer sympathetic to the Baader-Meinhof Group; and in the late 1950s and early 1960s he carried cash for the Front de libération nationale algérien [Algerian National Liberation Front], the guerrilla army fighting for independence from French rule in Algeria.

Guattari's activism was informed by his clinical practice as a psychotherapist in the private psychiatric clinic La Borde founded in 1953 by Jean Oury, with the aim of providing a radically new form of care which 'de-institutionalized the institution'.[18] At La Borde all staff, including cooks and cleaners, participated in providing therapy for the patients, many of whom were psychotic, and all staff, including doctors and nurses, participated in the maintenance of the hospital. 'What we're trying to do', Guattari explained in a note to Deleuze, is 'upset the caste imaginary that marks these patients, nurses and doctors (not to mention all the numerous subcastes!)' (AOP, 144/204). Guattari was enlisted by Oury because of his ability to organize collective action and thus help break down the barriers between staff and patients. Guattari received formal training in psychoanalysis from France's most important interpreter of Freud, Jacques Lacan, achieving the status of *analyste membre* in 1969. Although he remained a member of Lacan's school, the Ecole freudienne de Paris, until its dissolution in 1980 shortly before the master's death, Guattari's relationship to Lacan and Lacanian psychoanalysis was at best ambivalent.

The publication of Guattari's notebooks, *The Anti-Oedipus Papers*, has made it clear just how strained relations were between them, especially after the publication of *Anti-Oedipus* (even though that work was in the words of its authors designed to save Lacan from the Lacanians). Indeed, even before it was published Lacan was distressed by its possible contents and according to Guattari's journal put pressure on him to give him a copy of the manuscript. Guattari had to refuse because Deleuze, whose relation with Lacan wasn't as personal, only wanted to show Lacan the text when it was finished.[19] Deleuze and Lacan clearly regarded each other as rivals, as is evident in the fact that they deliberately scheduled their seminars at the same time, compelling students to choose between them. That Deleuze saw himself as the clear winner in their struggles can be seen in his tart remark that in writing *Anti-Oedipus* they'd tried to give Lacan some 'schizophrenic help'. By which he means eliminating Lacan's signature conceptual innovations, his notions of structure, the symbolic order, the signifier, and so on, which in Deleuze's unequivocal phrase are 'thoroughly misguided' (N, 14/25).

The collaboration between Deleuze and Guattari is often described as a meeting of opposites, the love story between a wasp and an orchid as one writer has put it.[20] But despite superficialities, this is clearly false inasmuch as it implies the one completes or complements the other. Moreover this myth, for that is clearly what it is, has had a rather pernicious effect. Guattari is variously treated as the junior partner and his contribution either downplayed or ignored altogether (and almost all commentators on Deleuze, myself included, have been guilty at one time or another of writing 'Deleuze' when really they meant 'Deleuze and Guattari'), or worse, the corruptor of Deleuze, and condemned to take the fall for all that is strange, disturbing or simply incomprehensible in their writings. I can but agree with Gary Genosko that something must be done to address the confiscation of Guattari's contribution, though I confess I'm at a loss as to what that might be.[21]

MAY '68

It is often said, on the authority of the authors' own words, that *Anti-Oedipus* is a May '68 book. But what does that mean? As Kristin Ross argues in her history of the events of May and its influence on French intellectual life, *May '68 and its Afterlives*, the meaning of May '68, one of the largest mass movements in history, was never straightforward or obvious, even to its participants, who were in any case very far from being uniform in their backgrounds, opinions, politics and motives.[22] Neither Deleuze nor Guattari are included in Ross's pantheon of thinkers, activists and writers whose 'intellectual and political trajectories' can be traced back to May '68.[23] At first glance, this might seem an injustice because after all it is not as though Deleuze and Guattari did not involve themselves in the events of May, particularly Guattari who took part in the infamous occupation of the Théâtre de l'Odéon. However, there is more than a grain of truth in Ross's verdict. By their own admission, Deleuze and Guattari were blindsided by May '68; it took them both by surprise and left them floundering for a response.[24] But, having said that, I see no reason to go along with Ross in thinking that Deleuze and Guattari's concepts of desire and becoming cannot be used to account for what happened that May.[25]

The difficulty Deleuze and Guattari had in forming a response to the events of May can be seen in the very texture of the work they produced together, especially its frequently bemoaned complexity. They were as troubled by the actualities of May '68 as they were excited by its possibilities and this ambivalence clearly shapes their theory of desire which tries to account for the contradictory currents of political thought and action that events like May '68 bring into stark relief.[26] Deleuze and Guattari were stirred by the possibility for change May '68 seemed to betoken, namely the liberation of desire itself, but they were also highly sceptical of the doctrinal turn that accompanied it, which seemed to them to promise the incarceration of desire all over again. They were particularly opposed to the Left Bank Maoism that blossomed that spring like the proverbial hundred flowers. They rejected the idea that May '68 constituted a first or preliminary stage in a longer struggle that would culminate in the installation of a new state apparatus.[27] 'It would be strange', Guattari remarked, 'to rely on a party or state apparatus for the liberation of desire.' (CY, 62).

If it is legitimate to say *Anti-Oedipus* is a May '68 book however, then it is because it was in a spirit of mutual ambivalence and uncertainty about May '68 that the two thinkers first came together in 1969. '[I]t was as less a question of pooling knowledge than the accumulation of our uncertainties and, even a certain distress in the face of the turn of events after May '68.' (CY, 93). In other words, it is legitimate to say *Anti-Oedipus* is a May '68 book providing it is understood that Deleuze and Guattari were not 'soixante-huitards' or May 68ers and that their view of those events was quite different from the students and workers who put up barricades in the streets and tore up paving stones in search of the beach underneath. Their reticence regarding May '68 can partially be explained in generational terms inasmuch that Deleuze and Guattari saw themselves as belonging to the generation prior to the actual 68ers (if by that one means the students at the Sorbonne who provided the initial spark of protest that set the politically seismic events in motion). Their intellectual and political formation took shape during World War II and its aftermath and wears the scars of the defeat, occupation and liberation of France in its scepticism towards all forms of organized politics. As Guattari explained in an interview following the publication of *Anti-Oedipus* in France in 1972: 'We are part of a generation whose political consciousness was born in the enthusiasm and naivety of the Liberation, with its conspirational mythology of fascism.' He further qualified this remark by adding that the 'questions left hanging by the other failed revolution that was May '68 were developed for us based on a counterpoint that was all the more troubling because, like many others, we were worried about the future being readied for us, one that could make you miss the fascism of yore'. (CY, 94). In other words, Deleuze and Guattari were distrustful of the immodest and frequently hubristic claims that were made about what May '68 really meant, i.e., that it had somehow changed everything, but not opposed to it in principle as many of their generation in fact were.[28] Ten years later, in *A Thousand Plateaus*, they would lash out at the May '68 naysayers like Raymond Aron as follows:

[T]hose who evaluated things in macropolitical terms understood nothing of the event because something unaccountable was escaping. The politicians, the parties, the unions, many leftists, were utterly vexed; they kept repeating over and again that 'conditions' were not ripe. It was as though they had been temporarily deprived of the entire dualism machine that made them valid spokespeople. (ATP, 238/264)

As is obvious from the stridently anti-capitalist tone of *Anti-Oedipus*, Deleuze and Guattari were highly sympathetic to the utopian (i.e., world-transformative) dimension of the May '68 struggles, but they weren't ready to accept that the solution was an immediate transition to communism.

Liberated desire means desire that escapes the impasse of private fantasy: it is not a question of adapting it, socialising it, disciplining it, but of plugging it in in such a way that its process not be interrupted in the social body, and that its expression be collective. What counts is not the authoritarian unification, but rather a sort of infinite spreading: desire in the schools, the factories, the neighbourhoods, the nursery schools, the prisons, etc. It is not a question of directing, of totalising, but of plugging into the same plan of oscillation. As long as one alternates between the impotent spontaneity of anarchy and the bureaucratic and hieratic coding of a party organisation, there is no liberation of desire. (CY, 62)

There can be no denying that *Anti-Oedipus* is conceived as a revolutionary book, i.e., a book that wants to open our eyes to the potential for revolution in the realm of everyday life. But as the passage just cited makes clear, its definition of revolution doesn't include taking power.[29] It doesn't mean overturning one regime and then installing another regime and reforming government from top to bottom as the Maoists and Leninists demand. It wants no part of such programmes.

Revolution for Deleuze and Guattari means schizophrenizing the existing power structure, making it vibrate to a new rhythm, making it change from within, without at the same time becoming a schizophrenic. But they don't offer a model for a new society, save that it won't replicate the old repressions. Their argument is that we'll never get to that new society the militants of every persuasion claim their doctrine is leading us towards if we don't first of all shed our old habits, our old love of power, our manifold addictions to the exercise of force, our customary obsequiousness in the face of power, and so on. 'Schizoanalysis as such does not raise the problem of the nature of the socius to come out of the revolution; it does not claim to be identical with the revolution itself.' (AO, 415/456). Its only question is, 'Where will the revolution come from?' From start to finish, *Anti-Oedipus* is dominated by this single question:

Will it come in the person of a Castro, an Arab, a Black Panther, or a Chinaman on the horizon? A May '68, a home-grown Maoist planted like an anchorite on a factory smoke-stack? Always the addition of an axiom to seal off a breach that has been discovered; fascist colonels start reading Mao, we won't be fooled again; Castro has become impossible, even in relation to himself; vacuoles are isolated, ghettos created; unions are appealed to for help; the most sinister forms of 'dissuasion' are invented; the repression of interest is reinforced – but where will the new irruption of desire come from? (AO, 413/454)

Deleuze and Guattari's answer to this question, which we'll examine in more detail in the chapters to follow, is that the new irruption of desire must always come from within desire itself. Desire is revolutionary in itself, Deleuze and Guattari argue, but it is constantly being shackled to, or worse converted into interest, and as interest it is susceptible to capture, domestication and pacification. Their conviction, reiterated throughout *Anti-Oedipus*, is that 'capitalist society can endure many manifestations of interest, but not one manifestation of desire, which would be enough to make its fundamental structures explode, even at the kindergarten level.' (AO, 414/455). But pure manifestations of desire are rare, even in actual revolutionary situations.

> One cannot account for a revolutionary situation by a simple analysis of the interests of the time. In 1903 the Russian Social Democratic Party debated the alliances and organisation of the proletariat, and the role of the avant-garde. While pretending to prepare for the revolution, it was suddenly shaken up by the events of 1905 and had to jump on board a moving train. There was a crystallisation of desire on a wide social scale created by a yet incomprehensible situation. Same thing in 1917. (CY, 65)

By the same token, there are always groups in place to capitalize on the disruption to the social order revolution causes.

> Daniel Guérin has said some profound things about the revolution of 1789. The bourgeoisie never had any illusions about who its real enemy was. Its real enemy was not the previous system, but what escaped the previous system's control, and what the bourgeoisie strove to master in its turn. It too owed its power to the ruin of the old system, but this power could only be exercised insofar as it opposed everything else that in rebellion against the old system. The bourgeoisie has never been revolutionary. It simply made sure others pulled off the revolution for it. It manipulated, channelled, and repressed an enormous popular desire. (CY, 65)

The point not to be missed here is that one cannot use interest as a way of determining where the revolution will come from, but one must take interest into account when one considers the parallel problem of 'Who will betray the revolution?' And for Deleuze and Guattari, these two questions, 'Where will the revolution come from?' and 'How will it be betrayed?' are ultimately different sides of the same coin.

ALGERIA, VIETNAM, ITALY . . .

Apprehending *Anti-Oedipus* as a May '68 book is a useful way of focusing the multiple and multivalent impulses that went into writing it, but the limitations of this framing device are obvious.[30] It risks making it seem that *Anti-Oedipus* was a purely local affair, a single-shot response to a single-shot event that took place in Paris three decades ago. It is true to say, as I will discuss in more detail in the next chapter, that many of the debates *Anti-Oedipus* weighs into are patently Parisian in nature. Indeed, it spars more or less overtly with practically every leading light of the intellectual scene in Paris at that time, particularly Louis Althusser, Jacques Lacan and Lévi-Strauss. But having said that, it is also true to say that the debates inspired by the work of Althusser, Lacan and Lévi-Strauss, not to mention the theoretical upheavals provoked by Jean Baudrillard, Hélène Cixous, Jacques Derrida, Michel Foucault, Luce Irigaray, Julia Kristeva and Jean-François Lyotard, reverberated around the world, albeit in the hermetic confines of university English and French departments. Students from all over the world flocked to Paris in the late 1960s and early 1970s to sit at the feet of these master thinkers who in their unwillingness to accept at face value the received wisdom of the past, in any of the disciplines, appeared to offer not only a new way of thinking, but verily a whole new worldview. In the history of theoretical discourse, *Anti-Oedipus* appeared at the dawn of a decade that was, as Fredric Jameson has put it, 'essentially French'.[31] However, the fact that theory had become or was becoming global in its distribution at this point does not prove that its production was anything other than a purely local affair. For that reason it is worth looking at May '68 itself and asking whether or not it was the purely local affair it appears to be to the untutored eye. Anticipating the discussion to follow, I want to propose the following corollary to my initial claim that it is legitimate to treat *Anti-Oedipus* as a May '68 book: It is legitimate to treat *Anti-Oedipus* as a May '68 book to the extent that May '68 itself is treated as a complex, multiply determined event whose place in history is far from settled.

Bernardo Bertolucci's highly stylized film about May '68, *The Dreamers* (2003), is a vivid illustration of the narrow, exclusively Parisian image of the events that has to be overturned if we are to see things in their proper historical light. Bertolucci depicts May '68 as a student protest, which is how it began, but its significance to history derives from the fact that it soon became a nationwide protest involving more than 9 million striking workers. The effects of the strikes are made apparent to us in the film in the form of mounds of uncollected garbage mouldering in stairwells and on street corners, but the striking workers themselves are never shown. Moreover, Bertolucci makes it seem the student protests began in the privileged cloisters of the Latin Quarter, and not, as was actually the case, in the functionalist towers of the new universities in the outlying immigrant slum areas of Nanterre and Vincennes, where students were provided 'with a direct "lived" lesson in uneven development'.[32] According to the great Marxist philosopher Henri Lefebvre, it was this daily 'experience' of the callousness of the state that radicalized the students and provided the catalyst for their connection to workers' movements.[33] Secondly, through the vehicle of its twin brother and sister protagonists Isabelle (Eva Green) and Theo (Louis Garrel), both in their late teens or early twenties and still living at home with their relatively well-to-do parents, it depicts the students who took part in May '68 as naïve, self-absorbed and perverted. Cocooned in their own fantasy world concocted from fragments of movies and books, Isabelle and Theo are a postmodern version of Ulrich and Agathe.[34] They meet an American exchange student, Matthew (Michael Pitt), and invite him join them. When their parents go away, they are able to indulge their whims uninhibitedly and the scene is set for a clichéd romp through the three staples of 1960s counterculture, namely sex, drugs and rock'n'roll. They take bubble baths together and get stoned on hash; Matthew and Isabelle make love on the kitchen floor while Theo fries an egg and looks on with Brechtian disinterest; they drink papa's fine wine straight from the bottle and debate movies and politics long into the night as though nothing else mattered. They ignore the world outside.

Matthew soon upsets their idyllic universe by accusing them both of being unworldly: Isabelle because she's never been out on a real 'date' and Theo because of his starry-eyed romanticization of the Chinese Red Guards. It all begins when Isabelle demands that he shave his pubic hair as a sign of love. He refuses because the demand is in his view nothing but a silly game, an infantalizing gesture that proves their disconnection from the reality of what is going on around them. He tells them both 'there's something going on out there, I can feel it', but neither Isabelle nor Theo seem to care. Their political awakening comes soon enough though in the form of a brick thrown through their apartment window. The brick literally shatters their world, but also saves their lives too. Awakening after another of their orgiastic episodes, Isabelle finds a cheque written by her parents and realizes that they must have been in the apartment and therefore witnessed their dishabille state and perhaps guessed at their decadent behaviour – the three of them are naked, sleeping side by side in a tent Isabelle erected in the living room. Mortally ashamed, Isabelle decides to kill herself and Theo and Matthew as well, so she switches on the gas and lays down between the two boys and readies herself for death. It is at this point that the window is broken. The intrusion of the street into their self-enclosed fantasy world is thus presented as a life-saving event. The brick breaks the spell of self-indulgence they've all been under and suddenly both Isabelle and Theo realize something is going on outside and that it does concern them, does interest them, and is more important than their fantasy world. The three of them rush first to the balcony to witness the events below and then to the street to join in. But here the happy trio split up because only Isabelle and Theo are willing to take part. Matthew, a self-proclaimed pacifist, turns his back on them. Having urged them both to take note of what is going on outside, Matthew recoils in horror when he sees Theo with a Molotov cocktail in his hands and refuses to join them when they rush hand in hand towards the fray. Bertolucci's last act then is to make May '68 an exclusively French affair, but also wrongheaded and needlessly violent.

Kristin Ross's account of May '68 takes us in precisely the opposite direction to Bertolucci. She is anxious that we see that May '68 was not just a student protest, and that those involved were anything but naive (in the sense of being unaware of history), and perhaps most importantly that it was part of a longer chain of events that stretched far beyond Paris. To begin with, Ross argues for an enlargement of the timeframe in which the events are considered, not just beyond the month of May itself, which as she shows (and Bertolucci's film exemplifies) restricts the events to a limited series of goings-on in the Sorbonne, but back two decades to the start of the Algerian War. This, in turn, enables her to argue that May '68 'was not a great cultural reform, a push toward modernisation, or the dawning sun of a new individualism. It was above all *not* a revolt on the part of the sociological category "youth".'[35] It was rather the revolt of a broad cross-section of workers and students of all ages who had grown up with and witnessed the sickening brutality of the Gaullist regime's failed attempt to deny Algeria its independence. 'Algeria defined a fracture in French society, in its identity, by creating a break between the official "humanist" discourse of that society and French practices occurring in Algeria and occasionally within France as well.'[36] It was impossible to reconcile the ideal of a benevolent welfare state espoused by France's leaders with the truncheon-wielding reality of the hegemonic state, except perhaps in oedipal terms by casting President de Gaulle in the role of father and relegating the protestors to the rank of children. *Anti-Oedipus* is of course directed against this pseudo-psychoanalytic account of the events and indeed Deleuze and Guattari argue that it was precisely the example of Algeria that makes it clear that politics cannot be reduced to an oedipal struggle. 'It is strange', they write, 'that we had to wait for the dreams of the colonised peoples in order to see that, on the vertices of the pseudo triangle, mommy was dancing with the missionary, daddy was being fucked by the tax collector, while the self was being beaten by the white man.' (AO, 105–6/114).

What Fanon's work showed us, Deleuze and Guattari go on to suggest, is that every subject is directly coupled to elements of their

> historical situation – the soldier, the cop, the occupier, the collaborator, the radical, the resister, the boss, the boss's wife – who constantly break all triangulations, and who prevent the entire situation from falling back on the familial complex and becoming internalised in it. (AO, 107/116)

As Belden Fields writes, the Algerian War was a crucial stimulus for the radicalization of French students in the 1960s because it delegitimized the structures of the state. 'The educational system, for instance, came to be viewed as a conduit funnelling young people into military bureaucracies to fight imperialist wars, or into capitalist bureaucracies, whether public or private, to earn a living as a supporting cog in a system of repressive privilege.'[37] Jean-Paul

Belmondo, 'the doomed anti-hero' of Jean-Luc Goddard's path-breaking film of 1960, *À bout de souffle* [*Breathless*], is usually taken as the 'screen representative of that young generation of Frenchmen condemned to serve, suffer, and even die in Algeria'.[38] This perceived lack of control over their own destiny, even among the relatively privileged classes to which the majority of students actually belonged, coupled with the oppressive archaism of the educational system itself, and indeed the state structure as a whole, generated among radicalized youth a powerful sense of empathy with all victims of the state. The students saw themselves as being in solidarity with factory workers, despite the fact that their destiny was to be the managers who would one day have to 'manage' these selfsame workers. In other words, in spite of the fact that their class interests were different, the students and the workers were nonetheless able to find a point of common interest in their dispute with the state. The usual divide and conquer tactics the state relies on to stratify the population and ensure that precisely this type of connection between strata doesn't occur failed spectacularly. It failed because the state was unable, at least in the first instance, to present itself as something other than a huge, oppressive monolithic edifice determined to stamp out dissent with an iron fist. Unfortunately, the French Communist Party, still a very strong and widely supported institution, was tarnished by its 'pragmatic' response to the war – the party line, that the war should be ended by negotiated settlement, was strictly enforced, with the result that it too came to be seen as ossified and antiquated and of little relevance to the needs of the present generation.[39] Deleuze and Guattari clearly shared this view; their frequent anti-reformist remarks should be seen as directed at the French Communist Party.

Ross's second move is to argue for an enlargement of the geographical framework in which the events are considered, not just beyond the Latin Quarter to the outer suburbs of Paris, but beyond France altogether to still another of its former colonies, namely Vietnam, which having rid itself of its French masters in the 1950s was then in the process of expelling the American pretenders.

> In its battle with the United States, with the worldwide political and cultural domination the United States had exerted since the end of World War II, Vietnam made possible a merging of the themes of anti-imperialism and anti-capitalism; the theoretical justification was loosely supplied by Maosim.[40]

In fact, the events themselves were sparked by an incident – a window of the American Express building on rue Scribe in Paris was broken – that occurred as part of a student protest against the war in Vietnam on 20 March 1968. The irruption of student protest at Nanterre two days later was in part provoked by the heavy-handedness of the police response to the anti-Vietnam march. The students at Nanterre rallied themselves under the banner of 'Mouvement du 22 mars', deliberately recalling Castro's 'July 26th Movement' commemorating the attack on Moncada fortress and the start of the insurrection against Batista. 'Vietnam thus both launched the action in the streets as well as brought under one umbrella a number of groups – the CVN [Comité Viêt-nam national] was dominated by Trotskyists, the CVB [Comité Viêt-nam de base] by Maoists – as well as previously unaffiliated militants working together.'[41] For the protesters, students and workers alike, Vietnam made manifest processes that were thought to be merely latent in the West. For one thing, it revealed both the inherent violence of the postmodern capitalist state and the lengths to which it is prepared to go in order to preserve its power. It demonstrated a willingness on the part of the powerful to use violence against the powerless to defend the *status quo*.[42] Vietnam also revealed the vulnerability of the super state and its susceptibility to a 'revolution from below' (DI, 213/297). Sartre, for one, was convinced that the true of origin of May '68 was Vietnam because the example of Vietnamese guerrillas winning a war against a vastly superior force, albeit at the cost of an enormous loss of life, extended the domain of the possible for Western intellectuals who otherwise thought of themselves as powerless in the face of the state.[43]

More concretely, French workers whose livelihoods were threatened by a process we know today as globalization, the process whereby local markets are forcibly opened to global competitors, saw themselves as victims of American imperialism too. Deleuze and Guattari were keenly aware of the high cost the structural adjustments (to use the purposefully dry language of economists):

If we look at today's [1972] situation, power necessarily has a global or total vision. What I mean is that every form of repression today [repression actuelles], and they are multiple, is easily totalised, systematised from the point of view of power: the racist repression against immigrants, the repression in factories, the repression in schools and teaching, and the repression of youth in general. We mustn't look for the unity of these forms of repression only in reaction to May '68, but more so in a concerted preparation and organisation concerning our immediate future. Capitalism in France is dropping its liberal, paternalistic mask of full employment; it desperately needs a 'reserve' of unemployed workers. It's from this vantage point that unity can be found in the forms of repression I already mentioned: the limitation of immigration, once it's understood we're leaving the hardest and lowest paying jobs to them; the repression in factories, because now it's all about once again giving the French a taste for hard work; the struggle against youth and the repression in schools and teaching, because police repression must be all the more active now that there is less need for young people on the job market. (DI, 210/294)

On this point, Ross argues that the geographical boundary of the events of May needs to be widened to encompass Italy because the political convulsions wrought by the first stages of globalization were nowhere in Europe felt more keenly.[44] The striking Fiat workers' slogan 'Vietnam is in our factories!' made the connection to American imperialism explicit. This is, then, Ross's third move: she argues for a redefinition of the sociological frame in which the events are considered. May '68 would not have been the event it was if the protest action had been confined to either the students or the workers or even the farmers. It was the fact that these groups, as well as many others, found it possible and necessary to link up with each other that resulted in the extraordinary event we know as May '68. But, and this is Ross's main point, none of these groups – students, workers, farmers, etc. – can be treated as pre-existing, self-contained, homogeneous entities. As for the encounters between these heterogeneous groups, they obviously cannot be treated in the same way that one might regard the actions of states agreeing by treaty to work together for the sake of a common interest. Ross suggests that the process might better be described as 'cultural contamination' and argues that it 'was encounters with people different from themselves – and not the glow of shared identity – that allowed a dream of change to flourish'.[45] Ross's purpose, however, is not to assert the primacy of the individual, or indeed the primacy of difference, two moves which as Jameson has shown in his various critiques of Anglo-American cultural studies lead inexorably to political paralysis. By repudiating both the collective and the same under the utterly misconceived banner of 'anti-totalization', cultural studies has for all practical intents and purposes divested itself of two of the most basic prerequisites for politics, namely the potential for a common action and the identification of a common aim.[46] Well aware of the pitfalls of valorizing the individual at the expense of the collective, the different at the expense of the same, Ross argues for an approach to the sociological dimension of May '68 that is perfectly attuned to Deleuze and Guattari's work.[47]

Ultimately for Deleuze and Guattari, accounting for May '68 necessitated a complete rethinking of political concepts like power, power relations, groups, group identity, the event, and so on, and insofar as it takes up this challenge, *Anti-Oedipus* is appropriately described as a May '68 book.

CHAPTER 2

OVERVIEW OF THEMES

Everything begins with Marx, continues on with Lenin, and ends with the refrain, 'Welcome, Mr Brezhnev'.

Gilles Deleuze and Félix Guattari, *Anti-Oedipus*

The schizo is not revolutionary, but the schizophrenic process – in terms of which the schizo is merely the interruption, or the continuation in the void – is the potential for revolution.

Gilles Deleuze and Félix Guattari, *Anti-Oedipus*

In the long aftermath of May '68, an event which many French intellectuals came to think of as a 'failed revolt', the question of power – what it is, how it functions, who has it and who does not – was the principal concern of the majority of France's leading intellectuals. Along with the interrelated questions concerning the possibility of resistance and (more concretely) the possibility of political action itself, power was the uppermost concern of Louis Althusser, Alain Badiou, Etienne Balibar, Jean Baudrillard, Pierre Bourdieu, Cornelius Castoriadis, Hélène Cixous, Régis Debray, Jacques Derrida, Michel Foucault, Luce Irigaray, Julia Kristeva, Henri Lefebvre, Jean-François Lyotard, Nicos Poulantzas, Jacques Rancière and Paul Virilio. Very far from homogeneous in their political and philosophical allegiances, though most would own to a Left-orientation, providing it was clear that didn't mean they were Marxists (or, in the case of Althusser and Althusserians like Balibar and Rancière, they would own to a Left-orientation providing it was understood that meant they were a very particular type of Marxist), there is a surprising degree of consistency across the quite diverse body of work produced by these writers in the decade after May '68 concerning the question of power.

There was, for instance, broad acceptance of the idea that power is not a simple matter of coercion or repression, the dominance of one group of people over another. It was generally agreed that contemporary society cannot be understood as the product or the expression of a powerful ruling elite exercising influence over a powerless majority. Moreover, there was broad agreement that power resides in the ordinary, that tradition, law, language and the way we organize our daily lives is directly and indirectly inflected by the operations of power. Similarly, there was a general acceptance of the proposition that power requires a degree of complicity on the part of the ruled to function, but disagreement on the question of how this was achieved. All theorists mentioned agree that the situation in which the planet finds itself today is parlous, to say the least, and they more or less agree on the cause, namely capitalism; what's more, they all agree things are in desperate need of change, but they disagree – often quite vehemently – as to how this change might be achieved. The debate that raged in respect to this last question concerned power directly inasmuch that the central point of contention was whether or not change could be achieved without forcibly taking power through some kind of revolutionary action.

Anti-Oedipus was lobbed into this fray like an intellectual cluster bomb – it had multiple targets, from the primacy of the signifier in linguistics to the dependency on lack in psychoanalysis, but its primary objective was (as Michel Foucault astutely points out in his highly influential preface to the English translation) to caution us against the fascist inside, the desire to seize power for oneself. The principal thesis of *Anti-Oedipus*, around which its many conceptual inventions turn, is that revolution is not primarily or even necessarily a matter of taking power. Insofar as taking power means preserving all the old institutions and ideas in which power is invested it could even be said that revolutions of this type are actually counter-revolutionary in purpose and intent because they change nothing essential. By the same token, Deleuze and Guattari were concerned about the allure of power, its apparent ability to drive us to desire to be placed under its yoke. The most important political question, as far as Deleuze and Guattari are concerned, is how it is possible for desire to act against its interest. In *Forget Foucault*, the late Jean Baudrillard's waspish polemic against everything that was thought 'fashionable' in theory in France in the 1970s, states that in Deleuze and Guattari's work 'desire's reversion into its own repression is inexplicable'.[1] His point is that if desire is such a powerful, liberatory force, then how is it possible that it ever came to be repressed in the first place. This is emblematic of a great many of the negative responses to Deleuze and Guattari's work. It betrays a significant misunderstanding of their project as a whole and of their concept of desire in particular.

Shortly before the appearance of *Anti-Oedipus*, the French cultural affairs journal *L'Arc* published a lengthy special issue dedicated to Deleuze's work. Wedged in amongst the criticisms and encomiums of various luminaries, there is a marvellous 'conversation' between Foucault and Deleuze pointedly entitled 'Intellectuals and Power'. It first appeared in English in 1977 in *Language, Counter-Memory, Practice*, a collection of Michel Foucault's interviews and essays edited by Donald Bouchard, and for that reason it is usually read by Anglo-American Foucauldians who treat it as a conveniently short exposition of Foucault's ideas on power in general and the role of the intellectual in particular. Perhaps for the same reason Anglo-American Deleuzians, with the signal exception of Michael Hardt, have given it relatively little attention, though I would suggest it can just as profitably be treated as a conveniently short exposition of Deleuze's ideas on power in general and the role of the intellectual in particular.[2] Indeed, inasmuch as Deleuze clearly uses the conversation to give notice of both the main themes and the principal critical targets of his forthcoming book, *Anti-Oedipus*, it might even be said to be the more concrete of the two. Deleuze pinpoints three 'areas of concern' that taken together adumbrate the schizoanalytic project as a whole as it would be articulated in *Anti-Oedipus*. Firstly he challenges the nature of the relation between theory and praxis, arguing that the latter is neither simply an extension of the former nor its inspiration; then he challenges the centrality of interest in understanding the operation of power; and lastly he emphasizes the importance of the microphysics of power and the potency of the powerless's demands.

Theory, Deleuze insists, 'is exactly like a tool box. It has nothing to do with the signifier . . . A theory has to be used, it has to work. And not just for itself.' (DI, 208/290).[3] He goes on to suggest that 'theory is by nature opposed to power', but its ability to oppose power is severely curtailed if it becomes too fixed in either its method or its object (DI, 208/291). For this reason, Deleuze rejects the idea of reform in favour of revolution, although it must be made clear that by the latter he does not mean a militant overthrow of a governing body. Perhaps most interestingly of all, Deleuze short-circuits the expected relation between theory and praxis. 'Praxis', he says, 'is a network of relays from one theoretical point to another, and theory relays one praxis to another.' But, he adds, a 'theory cannot be developed without encountering a wall, and praxis is needed to break through.' (DI, 206/288). He goes on then to give the example of Foucault's work on prisons which began by offering a theoretical account of the penal system but soon felt the necessity, as Deleuze puts it, of creating a relay to enable the imprisoned to speak for themselves. But, he insists, the GIP, Foucault's practical mechanism for enabling the prisoners to speak for themselves, was never a matter of the application of a theory. It was, rather, in language that is familiar to us from the later *A Thousand Plateaus*, a matter of multiplicity.[4]

> For us, the intellectual and theorist have ceased to be a subject, a consciousness that represents or is representative. And those involved in political struggle have ceased to be represented, whether by a party or union that would in turn claim for itself the right to be their conscience. Who speaks and acts? It's always a multiplicity, even in the person who speaks or acts. We are all groupuscules. (DI, 207/289)

THEORY AND PRAXIS

Deleuze's hypothesis is that hitherto most theories of power, particularly those developed by the Left, treat it as a problem of interests – power is consolidated in the hands of a ruling class and exercised according to a set of protocols that best serve their interests. The US invasion of Iraq in 2003, for instance, was blatantly in the interest of the ruling elite in the US inasmuch as it offered a tremendous opportunity for personal and corporate enrichment by pushing up the price of oil and providing a colossal windfall of lucrative 'no contest' and virtually 'no oversight' reconstruction contracts to swell the coffers without providing any tangible benefits for the Iraqi people footing the bill. In actual fact, not only has the ocean of money poured into reconstruction in Iraq failed to provide any benefit to the Iraqi people, in many cases it has worsened their situation. As British journalist Patrick Cockburn points out in his pungent account of the US occupation of Iraq, despite the expenditure of hundreds of millions of dollars, basic civic infrastructure such as power, water and sewage is still well below prewar levels four years after the official cessation of hostilities. Ironically, the American-led reconstruction of Baghdad has proceeded much less efficiently and effectively than did Saddam Hussein's regime following the first Gulf War.[5] When faced with such egregious examples of the (mis-)use of power, it is, as Deleuze puts it, perfectly obvious who exploits, who profits, and who governs (DI, 212/296). Yet, having said that, we are still faced with an important problem:

> how does it happen that those who have little stake in power follow, narrowly espouse, or grab for some piece of power? Perhaps it has to do with *investments*, as much economic as unconscious: there exist investments of desire which explain that one can if necessary desire not against one's interests, since interest always follows and appears wherever desire places it, but desire in a way that is deeper and more diffuse than one's interest. (DI, 212/296)

The problem of power is not only more complicated than the question of whose interests are being served it is also poorly formed if it is formulated only in terms of interest because there are many other varieties of power at work besides interest.

For Deleuze, the only adequate way of posing the question of power is in terms of desire. But one has to first of all abandon the old binaries that distinguish between the powerful and the powerless, those who have power and the freedom to exercise it and those who do not, because such rigid separations blind us to the real complexity of power relations. Power is a highly variegated substance with both a consolidated (molar) and dispersed (molecular) form. Consolidated and dispersed are not simply new codewords for powerful and powerless, but a reconfiguration of our understanding of how power actually works into the language of process. Every substance has both a consolidated and a dispersed dimension, depending on how you look at it. To the naked eye the human body is a self-contained whole made up of solid state organs and limbs, but under the microscope it is a vast multiplicity of cells which are made up of even more microscopic entities which rely on the pre-existence of still smaller entities and so on to infinity. The body never ceases to be the body, regardless of how infinitesimal our gaze is, just as the cells composing our body never cease in their being when we look up from the microscope. This is not to say that these two per-spectives on the body are either arbitrary or merely notional because the reality is that there is a very real tension between the molar and the molecular that Deleuze and Guattari ascribe to the 'law of large numbers'. Take the example of the elite athlete: if they over-train, or push it too hard in competition, then the exertions of the molar body, i.e., the body seen as a whole, lead to a rapid breakdown of the molecular body; but, by the same token, it is precisely the condition of the body in its molecular dimension that determines whether an athlete will be great or not – they triumph or fail according to whether their muscle fibres are composed one way and not another. It might be said that the reason philosophy has been unable to answer the question of 'what can a body do?' is that it hasn't found the right way to pose the question so that it takes account of the body's inherent multiplicity (ATP, 283/314). This is effectively Deleuze's complaint about the standard conception of power as interest: it doesn't take account of power's multiplicity.

Politics, it follows, depends very much on how you look at things. Naomi Klein's account of the potency and the vulnerability of the corporations that seem to stand astride the postmodern world like latter-day Titans is an excellent illustration of this point. By turns, the brand is the expression of the power of the corporation to shape the very look, feel, taste and texture of the contemporary world, and, for this very reason, the weakest link in the multinational chain. Irrespective of how lean its manufacturing and distribution net-works are giant companies are vulnerable at the point of sale: if the brand is tarnished the multinational corporation can be brought to its knees by the simple fact of their products failing to sell in sufficiently large numbers to sustain their machinic momentum. If Disney loses its homely image or Coke its sense of fun, then the unthinkable may happen: people may very well stop buying their products. This is what makes the corporations such paranoid vigi-lantes when it comes to the control of their image. It explains, too, why they are so litigious in protecting their images – image is every-thing. This is the one iota of hope Klein offers readers of *No Logo*, which is otherwise an unremitting tale of woe recounting the suc-cessive loss of the authenticity, originality and indeed vitality of global cultures. Culture-jamming, a kind of guerrilla aesthetic which attacks the image itself by altering it in such a way as to trans-form it into an 'X-ray of the subconscious' of the underpinning sales message, is in its aggressive 'writing back' the expression of the power of the otherwise powerless.[6] When feminist culture-jammers scrawl 'feed me' beside images of emaciated supermodels and emphasize their point that this conception of beauty is unhealthy by transforming the models' deathly vacant faces into hideous skulls by blacking out their eyes and teeth, they shatter the molar power of the message 'buy me'. The net result of their attack is a molecular multiplicity of messages, only some of which retain their original appeal. Molecularized in this way, the advertisement loses some, perhaps even its entire efficacy, as potential consumers contemplate the real cost of the commodity they are considering purchasing. Culture-jamming unleashes the pent-up negativity, scepticism and cynicism capitalism simultaneously induces and contains.

But to read Klein in a properly Deleuzian manner one has to read the hopeful chapters on culture-jamming alongside the rather more sobering chapters on the expropriation of cool because only then does one see that the molecularizing power of culture-jamming is precisely what enables the molarizing recuperation of dissent implicit in the commodification of cool. Cool-hunting, the practice of scouring the ghetto and the barrio for new style ideas and turning them into the next 'latest thing' in fashion, is the flip-side of culture-jamming: it converts the often facetious, ironic or parodic uses of clothing found in disenfranchized 'have-not' communities into commodities for the 'have-yachts'. The baggy jeans hanging so low they reveal the waistband of the underwear beneath which Calvin Klein made its signature image in the late 1990s was in its original 'gangsta' context a sign that its wearer had been incarcerated and functioned semiotically as an assertion of 'street' credibility. Now, though, in its decontextualized and suburbanized mode it is simply an excuse to reveal a hitherto hidden label. As Klein herself argues, cool-hunting is an extremely cynical exercise which 'feeds off the alienation at the heart of America's race relations: selling white youth on their fetishisation of black style, and black youth on their fetishisation of wealth'.[7] In *The Conquest of Cool*, Thomas Frank demonstrates that this cynicism conceals the corporate world's deep-seated reliance on the so-called counterculture to create new markets. Capitalism willingly turns youthful rebellion into a business opportunity: thus the 1960s refusal to wear standardized clothes, i.e., the same old boring grey flannel suit father wore, and the same buttoned-up pinafore dress mother wore, created the opening for what we today think of as simply fashion and the endless parade of apparently radical, new forms of chic.[8] In spite of itself, the culture of dissent turned out to serve the interests of the very thing it was protesting against, namely the archly conservative order of global capitalism. The conclusion Deleuze and Guattari draw from this is not, however, the gloomy idea at the heart of 'cynical reason' (Sloterdijk) that capital always triumphs and therefore nothing can be done to change things. On the contrary, they conclude that capitalism's very facility for unleashing and containing change means that it is tapping into a highly unstable energy source, namely desire, which in their view is revolutionary by nature, and is therefore extremely vulnerable.[9]

RENOVATING PSYCHOANALYSIS

Deleuze and Guattari's schizoanalytic revolution hinges on their renovation of the psychoanalytic concept of the unconscious.[10] As will be seen in what follows, Deleuze and Guattari preserve this basic model of the unconscious; they even keep to Freud's tripartite way of thinking about it; but they change its internal dynamics. First of all, they reject the notion that it is the unconscious that pressures the conscious; on the contrary, they say, it is the conscious that pressures the unconscious (AO, 371/404). Instead of a model of the unconscious containing a host of unruly thoughts, a veritable 'aboriginal population in the mind' (as Freud put it, in one of his more unfortunate phrasings), constantly trying to penetrate the barrier between the two systems, what Deleuze and Guattari envision is something like a head full of unruly thoughts that have been made to look into the mirror by a domineering conscious only to be told they are something other than what they see.[11] These changes will become more apparent if we set them against the background of Freud's work.

Freud conceives the unconscious in three interrelated ways: dynamically, topographically and economically. However, it was not until his 1915 paper 'The Unconscious' that he brought these strands together in a systematic way. This same paper is credited by Deleuze and Guattari with the discovery of 'desiring-production', which as will become clear in what follows is the essential conceptual bedrock of their position. In a very provisional way, we can say it is simply their word for what Freud called 'das Es', adopting the term from Georg Groddeck, who in turn adopted it from his teacher Ernst Schweninger. Idiosyncratically, Freud's English translator rendered 'das Es' as 'Id' rather than 'It', which would have been more strictly correct, in order to be consistent with the use of the Greek word 'Ego' for 'I' with which it forms a complex binary pair.[12] But as Freud himself acknowledged, it was really Nietzsche who first gave the word the sense it has today.[13] Id is psychic energy in its raw state. Id is a force inside us which is by nature compulsive, driving, impersonal, hungry, insatiable, sexual, aggressive, creative and destructive – it lives in us, but we experience it as 'other'. In his *Introductory Lectures on Psychoanalysis*, written and delivered between 1915 and 1917, Freud describes the processes of the unconscious corresponding to the id as being like a rowdy guest one has ejected from a lecture theatre who nonetheless continues to hammer on the door even after his banishment causing such a ruckus that one is compelled to post a guard. This hypothesis is at the basis of all Freud's speculations concerning the formation and function of the mind. Slips of the tongue are simply instances of that rowdy guest evading the guard and making an unscheduled appearance in the conscious; while symptoms are simply the lengths we feel we must go to in order to avoid this same rowdy guest once and for all. Freud views the unconscious as an atavistic reservoir of dark passions that 'we' as civilized subjects of a modern society have learned to keep at bay. Civilization, as Freud understands it, by which he simply means any form of collective society, can only be had at the price of taming the 'Id'.

On this view of things, the conscious mind is beset by the constant pressure of what it perceives to be dark and disturbing thoughts and impulses it feels it must keep under wraps in the unconscious or cause unpleasure for itself, so it represses them in the unconscious. But this is precisely the view of the unconscious that Deleuze and Guattari reject. Therefore it is impossible to maintain that desiring-production is another word for id. Desiring-production is not simply id by another name as the ambiguous opening paragraph of *Anti-Oedipus* might seem to suggest; it is not, in other words, a reservoir of repressed desires applying pressure to a beleaguered ego.[14] Desiring-production cannot be equated with id, despite the apparent similarities, because on Freud's definition the id has no access to reality except through the agency of the ego's connection to what Freud calls the perception-conscious system, which is inconsistent with what Deleuze and Guattari say about the function of machines.[15] Machines, they say, connect us to reality. If a Freudian analogy is needed, then desiring-production would be functionally equivalent to the system of the unconscious *as a whole*. The crucial implication of this statement, which isn't immediately obvious, is that it is the 'faults' or 'glitches' in the *process* of desire that result in us winding up schizophrenic, neurotic or perverted or whatever. But this is perhaps the wrong way of putting it since Deleuze and Guattari do not offer a model or picture of what the system would like look if it were free of glitches, except in the negative extreme of death. Thus to be faulty is to be alive – our glitches make us who we are. And as Woody Allen might put it, we can neither live with them or without them. This explains why desiring-production is the effective category (which means something rather more specific than the translator's rendering of it as 'principal concern' – it refers to that part of the 'psychical apparatus' which is determining in relation to the other parts) of schizoanalysis – it is *not* at the level of desiring-machines, which are in their own way cognates of the Freudian notions of the drive and the symptom, that a schizoanalytic 'cure' is effected. The 'cure' is rather an affair of desiring-production, of getting it going and giving it somewhere to go other than into the void.

The whole of psychoanalysis stands on this assumption that there are types of thoughts or ideas that the conscious, forged in the crucible of contemporary social life as it is, cannot tolerate and is therefore obliged to repress. In the popular imagination, it is usually assumed that these thoughts are unrealizable sexual fantasies and though that isn't completely wrong it isn't the whole story either. The conscious not only represses illicit sexual desires, it also represses thoughts and ideas it deems illogical, irrational or impossible. For this reason the process of sorting through which ideas may pass into the conscious and which may not is variously known as 'censorship' and 'reality testing'. The unconscious, in all its aspects, is the source of these intolerable ideas and it is the job of the censors to keep them there. Freud describes his first conceptualization of the unconscious as dynamic because what he sought to register is the transformability of thoughts and ideas – they can be unconscious to begin with and later become conscious, just as they can be conscious to begin with and later become unconscious. The unconscious thought or idea is generally known as 'latent' because it is capable of becoming conscious. The psychoanalytic cure is effected by finding the means of clearing the way for the latent thought to become manifest. The assumption is that the latent thought sticks in the unconscious like a thorn in the flesh, constantly worrying away at us until it has broken through all the barriers and found its way to the conscious. But since we fear that above all, we are constantly exercised to find fresh ways of preventing this from happening. So having repressed the thought once, we repress it again, and moreover we repress those things which might remind us of the thing we've repressed. The first instance of repression Freud calls 'primal repression'; the second, ongoing repression, which takes aim at associations and reminders of the original repression, Freud calls 'repression proper'. In therapy, these repressions take the form of 'resistances', they are the impediments to the cure, which paradoxically enough has to undo all the repressions. Because the only way the idea-thorn we have repressed can be removed once and for all is by exposing it to light. It has to be made manifest by being put into words, which is why psychoanalysis is known as the 'talking cure'.

The incompleteness of this modelling of the unconscious is obvious: it doesn't account for where thoughts go when they become unconscious, nor does it account for why some thoughts and not others are condemned to confinement in the unconscious. These gaps would duly be filled by the addition of a topographic and then economic modelling of the unconscious. The topographic conception of the unconscious treats the unconscious and the conscious as distinct spatial realms. This spatialization of the unconscious has no correlate in the anatomy; it refers exclusively to the disposition of the psychical apparatus. Its purpose is to account for the hypothesis that thoughts and ideas are presented differently in each of the two domains: in the conscious system the thought or idea is presented along with the word belonging to it; whereas in the unconscious system the thought or idea is presented alone. As Freud observes, with respect to the symptoms of one of his most famous patients, the Wolf-Man, there is scant similarity at the level of the thing between squeezing a pimple and ejaculating and still less between a sock and a vagina, but verbally both pimples and penises can be said to 'spurt', while socks and vaginas can both be said to be 'dark holes'. The Wolf-Man's associations are thus dictated by a similarity at the level of words, not things, and this (Freud thinks) is how schizophrenia works: it is a loss of reality manifesting itself as the confusion of words for things.[16] The economic conceptualization of the unconscious, which completes the picture, is by far the most consequential of the three ways of conceiving the operations of the unconscious. In moving from the dynamic and topographic to the economic we shift from a qualitative to a quantitative model of the unconscious. On the economic view of things, unconscious thoughts are conceived as a quantity of psychic energy that is looking for an outlet to discharge itself – this is what Freud means by cathexis.

Deleuze and Guattari consider the turn toward Oedipus, which psychoanalysis made relatively late in its development (it was 'discovered' by Freud in 1897 in the course of the self-analysis that led to the writing of *The Interpretation of Dreams*, but wasn't generalized into a model of the unconscious until 1923 in *The Ego and the Id*), a 'long mistake' whose history they undertake to write. They consider it a mistake inasmuch that Freud's first discovery was 'the domain of free syntheses where everything is possible: endless connections, nonexclusive disjunctions, non-specific conjunctions, partial objects and flows'. (AO, 61/63). In other words, psychoanalysis *was* a form of schizoanalysis to begin with, but then took a wrong turning. In this respect, psychoanalysis is (they say) like the Russian Revolution; no one knows when it started to go bad, or how far one has to go back to locate the source or point of its wrong turning. 'To the Americans? To the First International? To the secret Committee? To the first ruptures, which signify renunciations by Freud as much as betrayals by those who break with him? To Freud himself, from the moment of "discovery" of Oedipus?' (AO, 62/64). The crucial point is that Freud was not unaware of desiring-production, indeed in Deleuze and Guattari's view he discovered it, but for some reason he chose to turn his back on it. In consequence of this decision, psychoanalysis became an instrument of repression, one that was all the more insidious for appearing to be the opposite of that, for appearing to liberate the discourse of the unconscious when in fact what it did was force it to speak in a language of myths and fantasies, never anything real. But the greater loss, and the greater mistake, as it were, was the compromising of the two correlates of Freud's initial discovery, namely the

> direct confrontation between desiring-production and social production, between symptomological and collective formations, given their identical nature and their differing régimes; and on the other hand, the repression that the social machine exercises on desiring-machines, and the relationship of psychic repression with social repression. (AO, 61/63)

The trouble is, once it is in place, Oedipus appropriates desiring-production's outputs for itself, which then appear as its products, making it seem that our symptoms, dreams, delusions, and so on, were Oedipal after all (AO, 63/66). The principal mistake, then, was to put the social beyond the reach of desire. This in turn rendered it unfit for a concrete connection with Marxism.

> [W]hat does it mean to say that Freud discovered Oedipus in his own self-analysis? Was it in his self-analysis, or rather in his Goethian classical culture? In his self-analysis he discovers something about which he remarks: Well now, that looks like Oedipus! (AO, 62/64)

As readers of Freud's *Interpretation of Dreams* are aware, Freud's rationale for focusing on the story of Oedipus is that Oedipus's destiny can only continue to move us some two thousand years after it was written because it expresses an eternal truth, something that our unconscious recognizes and responds to even if our conscious does not. 'His destiny', Freud writes, 'moves us only because it might have been ours – because the oracle laid the same curse upon us before our birth as upon him. It is the fate of all of us, perhaps, to direct our first sexual impulse towards our mother and our first hatred and our first murderous wish against our father. Our dreams convince us that this is so.'[17] This brief passage has inspired countless literary critics to respond to literature, and subsequently film and virtually all forms of aesthetic production, in a similar way: to assume that their response to the work expresses not merely a personal predilection or taste for such and such a piece, but rather an eternal truth about their humanity, their inner and as it were primordial desires beyond their knowing. Not only that, psychoanalysis assumes that our response to all aesthetic works is somehow a response to this one play by Sophocles, that regardless of what we're reading, listening to or looking at, it is always *as if* it were *Oedipus Rex*. 'And there is the essential thing: the reproduction of desire gives way to a simple representation, in the process as well as the theory of the cure.' (AO, 61/63–4). Psychoanalysis is obviously more sophisticated than this rough summary allows, but in the years since Freud first made his 'discovery' psychoanalysis has simply disguised this basic premise by transforming it into a structural model. Thus the supposedly Oedipal desire for our mother has been transposed into a structural desire for the forbidden; and our first murderous hatred toward our father has been transposed into a structural agency of prohibition that has been variously associated with authority figures in particular (such as bosses, generals, presidents and so forth) and the socially imposed regulation of conduct in general. In the process, Oedipus is doubled, or becomes in effect what Bateson referred to as a double-bind, because now it is either something we identify with and the cause of a 'crisis', or it is a symbolic structure into which we can insert ourselves only at the price of disavowing our innermost desires and hence the source of perpetual inner 'conflict' (AO, 90/98).

But just because Deleuze and Guattari are anti-representation, that doesn't mean they are somehow against the idea that literature can tell us anything about how the unconscious works. It is obvious from the opening pages of *Anti-Oedipus* that literature is very important to Deleuze and Guattari – the literary references always outnumber the clinical references when it comes to exemplifying what schizophrenia is like: for every Schreber there is an Artaud (who probably was schizophrenic himself, but nonetheless wrote literature rather than memoirs of his neurotic illness) and a Beckett; for every Wolf-Man there is a Nerval (who also was probably a schizophrenic, or at least a manic depressive) and a Büchner, and so on. These works by Artaud, Beckett, Büchner and Nerval (and we could add Michaux, Moritz, Proust and Rimbaud, to list only some of the most frequently cited) do not represent schizophrenia; they don't offer us representations of schizophrenia; they are, in Deleuze and Guattari's vernacular, schizophrenia 'in person'. It is not the author that is schizophrenic in other words, although that may also be the case, but the work itself. 'Engels demonstrated', they write, that

an author is great because he cannot prevent himself from tracing flows and causing them to circulate, flows that split asunder the catholic and despotic signifier of his work, and that necessarily nourish a revolutionary machine on the horizon. That's what style is, or rather the absence of style – asyntactic, agrammatical: the moment when language is no longer defined by what it says, even less by what makes it a signifying thing, but what it causes it to move, to flow, and to explode – desire. For literature is like schizophrenia: a process and not a goal, a production and not an expression. (AO, 145/158–9)

But, in their view, literature is a rare art, and one that is highly vulnerable to the destructive influence of capitalism. 'Every writer is a sellout. The only literature is that which places an explosive device in its package, fabricating a counterfeit currency, causing the superego and its form of expression to explode, as well as the market value of its form of content.' (AO, 146/160). It is not by accident that Deleuze and Guattari's one collaborative book specifically on literature, namely their book on Kafka, focuses on a writer who famously published virtually nothing in his own lifetime.[18] In published work, particularly in the case of successful authors like F. Scott Fitzgerald, another author Deleuze and Guattari very much admire, it becomes too difficult to separate out desire from the sticky entanglements of interest.

The difference between these two ways of approaching the unconscious (as reservoir of repressed thoughts and fantasies or as a productive process which gives rise to machines) can readily be seen by comparing Freud's account of Schreber's delirium with Deleuze and Guattari's. Whereas Freud insists that behind all the elements of Schreber's impressively complicated delusional world (replete with talking birds, an upper and lower god, as well as the constant threat of soul-murder), stand real people (usually his parents), Deleuze and Guattari argue that these are merely so many 'intensities' through which his delirium moves. Whereas psychoanalysis regards the content of delirium as constituting a rebus which can be decoded by reading it against the eternal puzzle-solution of the Oedipus complex, schizoanalysis argues that it has no content, just a constantly evolving grid of flows and break-flows (schizzes). Thus, to take only one example, Freud interprets Schreber's 'becoming-woman', his feeling that he must become a woman because the Order of Things requires him to do so for the salvation of the world, as an expression of his ambivalent feelings for his father, which according to the Oedipal model are a supposed to be a combination of resentment and supplication. Psychoanalysis takes the view that the son regards his father as a rival for the mother's affection. But the son also knows that the father is too powerful a rival to be deposed, so he tries instead to supplicate him by taking a passive attitude towards him, which for obvious reasons provokes resentment in the son.[19] Using the Oedipal template, Freud quickly finds confirmation of his thesis in Schreber's writing – God represents Schreber's psychiatrist Dr Flechsig, and in turn stands in for Schreber's father. But in doing so, he neglects the political and historical content of Schreber's delusion, reducing it all down to Oedipal metaphors (AO, 64/66; 98/107). Although Freud acknowledges that Schreber's father was an influential medical doctor famous throughout Germany for his advocacy of the virtues of exercise and the outdoors, he neglects to mention the bizarre orthopaedic machines for correcting posture and so forth that the good doctor patented (AO, 327/353). In contrast to Freud, then, Deleuze and Guattari play down the significance of the father and play up the significance of the political and historical content.

> The psychoanalyst tells us that the father is important precisely because Schreber doesn't talk about him. We reply that we have never seen a schizophrenic delirium that is not firstly about race, racism, politics, that does not begin in all directions from history, that does not involve culture, that does not speak of continents, kingdoms, and so forth. We state that the problem of delirium is not connected to the family, and concerns the father and mother only in a very secondary way, if it concerns them at all. (CY, 80)

Perhaps the main difference, though, between psychoanalysis and schizoanalysis is this: Freud maintains that there is a metapsychological cause to Schreber's illness (namely his homosexual feelings towards Dr Flechsig) whereas Deleuze and Guattari insist that its cause is organic. 'In this sense, we believe in a biochemistry of schizophrenia (in conjunction with a biochemistry of drugs), that will be progressively more capable of determining the nature' of this illness (AO, 93/100). With respect to delirium, Deleuze and Guattari very clearly take the view that the schizophrenic does not *decide* to see the world *that way*, nor can they *decide* not to see the world *that way*. 'The schizophrenic is a person who, for whatever reason has been touched off by a desiring flow which threatens the social order.' (CY, 222). Something 'clicks' in the schizophrenic and their psychical apparatus shifts into a kind of overdrive, generating ideas, images, thoughts and feelings of greater intensity than anything previously known or experienced. In consequence of this shifting of gears, their *process of production*, their way of processing and synthesizing data and stimuli (both internal and external), alters in its mode of operation.[20] Schizophrenia enacts a regime change in the mind. Confirmation of the inference that Deleuze and Guattari attribute an organic cause to schizophrenia can be found in three places: first, contrary to Freud, Deleuze and Guattari take the view that schizophrenia's symptoms aren't penetrable by interpretation; second, contrary to psychiatry, which views schizophrenia as abnormal, Deleuze and Guattari take the view that the schizo process is completely normal (it is not the schizophrenic process that makes the schizo ill, they argue, but the environment in which he or she finds himself); and third, as I've already mentioned, Deleuze and Guattari speak in favour of drug therapy (CY, 86; ATP 313/347). This last point is especially telling – there would be no point in attempting to treat schizophrenia with psychotropic drugs if it was caused simply by an unfavourable reaction to one's childhood, as if we were somehow sick from our childhood.

Freud concluded that Schreber's delusions amounted to a 'loss of reality', and proposed that this constituted one of the main symptoms of schizophrenia. He took Schreber's delusional world to mean that he was becoming disconnected from the 'real world' and thereby falling into a dark world of his own imagining.[21] And insofar as Schreber insisted that he had sunbeams in his ass, it is hard to see how or why one should refute Freud's conclusion. It seems patently obvious that Schreber's grip on reality was profoundly diminished. Yet Deleuze and Guattari argue that the opposite is the case – far from suffering a 'loss of reality', the schizophrenic suffers from 'too much reality', the operative word being 'suffers'. The schizophrenic 'suffers' from 'too much reality' in the sense that this experience can be and often is both painful and distressing; but they also 'suffer' from 'too much reality' in the technical sense that the experience is completely involuntary (CY, 86). This feeling, usually referred to in psychiatric and psychoanalytic discourse as 'psychosis', in which the impossible and the possible have fused into one continuous reality, is the clinical basis of Deleuze and Guattari's entire project (DI, 234/326). In *Anti-Oedipus* they narrate the lived experience of the passage to psychosis as a kind of 'breakthrough', as the breaching of the notional but nevertheless real wall separating reason from unreason. But, as they are always quick to add, it is a 'breakthrough' which carries with it the constant risk of a 'breakdown', which can take one of two forms: either a lapse into speechless catatonia, or an endless nonsensical jabbering – 'I am God I was not God I am a clown of God . . .' (AO, 86/92). Their hypothesis is that what we see through the cracks in the wall between reason and unreason caused by the irruption of the schizophrenic process are the operations of the unconscious at their most primitive, functional level, namely that of something they call 'desiring-production'. As we'll see in the next chapter, this is where the desiring-machines come into being; this is where the desiring-machines do their work.

CHAPTER 3

READING THE TEXT

We don't claim to have written a madman's book, just a book in which one no longer knows – and there is no reason to know – who exactly is speaking, a doctor, a patient, an untreated patient, a present, past, or future patient. That's why we used so many writers and poets; who is to say if they are speaking as patients or doctors – patients or doctors of civilisation.

Gilles Deleuze and Félix Guattari, 'In Flux'

Is it our fault that Lawrence, Miller, Kerouac, Burroughs, Artaud, and Beckett know more about schizophrenia than psychiatrists and psychoanalysts?

Gilles Deleuze, *Negotiations*

DESIRING-MACHINES

In the various interviews they gave following the publication of *Anti-Oedipus*, Deleuze invariably says that their starting point was the concept of the desiring-machine, the invention of which he attributes to Guattari. There is no record of how Guattari came up with the idea, but on the evidence of his recently published notebooks, *The Anti-Oedipus Papers*, his clinical experience at La Borde had a large part to play. As Deleuze tells it, Guattari came to him with an idea for a productive unconscious, built around the concept of desiring-machines. In its first formulation, though, it was judged by them both to be too structuralist to achieve the kind of radical breakthrough in understanding how desire functions that they were both looking for in their own ways. At the time, according to Deleuze, he was working – 'rather timidly' in his own estimation – 'solely with concepts' and could see that Guattari's ideas were a step beyond where his thinking had reached (N, 13/24). Unsurprisingly, Guattari's version of events concurs with Deleuze's, though he credits the latter with being the one whose thinking had advanced the furthest. Guattari describes himself as wanting to work with Deleuze both to make his break with Lacanian formulations more thoroughgoing and to give greater system and order to his ideas. But as we've already seen their collaboration was also always more than a simple exchange of ideas, each providing the other with something they lacked. They were both looking for a discourse that was both political and psychiatric but didn't reduce one dimension to the other. Neither seemed to think he could discover it on his own (N, 13/24). To put it another way, we could say that Deleuze and Guattari were both of the view that a mode of analysis that insists on filtering everything through the triangulating lens of daddy-mommy-me could not hope to explain either why or how May '68 happened, nor indeed why it went they way it did. The students at the barricades may have been rebelling against the 'paternal' authority of the state, but they were also rebelling against the very idea of the state and the former does not explain the latter.

The principal goal of *Anti-Oedipus* was to achieve a theoretical rapprochement between psychoanalysis and Marxism in order to create a new method of critical analysis (one better suited to the tenor of the times, as they saw things) which the authors provocatively refer to as either 'materialist psychiatry' or 'schizoanalysis' (the terms are used interchangeably). To achieve this goal, it had to accomplish two things:

1. introduce desire into the conceptual mechanism used to understand social production and reproduction, making it part of the very infrastructure of daily life;
2. introduce the notion of production into the concept of desire, thus removing the artificial boundary separating the machinations of desire from the realities of history.

These two objectives define the priorities of the first chapter.

Schizophrenic out for a stroll

The opening pages of *Anti-Oedipus* are undoubtedly the most obscure in the whole book. Yet we shouldn't let their apparent opacity deceive us into thinking they are without purpose or design. The case studies of Schreber, Lenz and Malone, with which *Anti-Oedipus* somewhat infamously opens, have three aims:

1. to distinguish between schizophrenia as process and schizophrenia as illness;
2. to identify the operative elements of the schizophrenic process;
3. to demonstrate that the schizophrenic process is the basic matrix of the unconscious.

Schizophrenia, Deleuze and Guattari say, is a 'harrowing, emotionally overwhelming experience, which brings the schizo as close as possible to matter, to a burning, living centre of matter' (AO, 21/26). However, their view is that it is not the disease process but the treatment which is the true cause of the catatonic zombies and ranting paranoiacs that haunt the popular imagination. The disease itself, providing its process isn't brought to an abrupt halt (through isolation in a lockdown ward), or allowed to turn in a void (through interminable analysis of the content of delusions), can give rise to tremendous flights of imagination and has undoubtedly been responsible for some of the greatest works of art throughout history. Thus the schizophrenic process is not the same thing as schizophrenia, the illness, which Deleuze and Guattari readily acknowledge can be a distressing and debilitating disease. Essentially, what Deleuze and Guattari want to demonstrate is this: the schizophrenic, in the full flight of delirium, reveals to us the true nature of desire as a synthetic process. The schizophrenic process, then, is Deleuze and Guattari's model of how desire works. 'Before being a mental state of the schizophrenic who has made himself into an artificial person through autism, schizophrenia is the process of the production of desire and desiring-machines.' (AO, 26/31–2). Deleuze and Guattari are not saying that everyone is really schizophrenic, albeit without being aware of it. And they do not intend to pulverize the subject beyond all measure or order as Perry Anderson pessimistically supposes.[1] Nor do they romanticize the schizophrenic as others have charged (N, 23/37). Rather, what they are saying is that we can learn a great deal from schizophrenic delirium because it lays bare the material processes of the unconscious. As I will show in more detail below, their argument is that schizophrenic delirium could not take the forms it does if the unconscious was not, as they put it, machinic. The distinction between schizophrenia as process and schizophrenia as illness is the necessary precondition for the next two points, namely the identification of the operative elements of the schizophrenic process and the mapping of those elements against the processes of the unconscious.

Regarding the second point – the identification of the operative elements of the schizophrenic process – the principal conclusion Deleuze and Guattari draw from the first three case studies (and reaffirm with every example that follows) is this: the schizophrenic is both *Homo natura* and *Homo historia*. What do they mean by this? As they themselves indicate, they are not saying schizophrenics are organically predisposed to an interest in nature; nor are they saying that an interest in nature can be used as a sign and symptom of the disease. 'We are not attempting to make nature one of the poles of schizophrenia. What the schizophrenic lives, both as an individual and as a member of the human species, is not at all any one specific aspect of nature, but nature as a *process of production*.' (AO, 3/9 translation modified, emphasis added). For instance, it is not Lenz's interest in rocks, metals, water and plants *per se* that signals the underlying presence of schizophrenia. More telling, in Deleuze and Guattari's view, is the way he regards these elements. It is how he sees things, not what he sees that is instructive.

Büchner's Lenz is obviously not the first artist to be inspired by the magnificence of the natural environment, or the first to wax so lyrically about it. But in contrast to other Romantic artists, who have similarly seen fit to make nature their subject, Lenz perceives in the natural elements a profound presence of Life, not just a strange and terrible beauty. Here Deleuze and Guattari take the opposite view to R.D. Laing who writes (speaking of Beckett's characters as it happens) that in the schizophrenic world 'there is no contradictory sense of the self in its "health and validity" to mitigate the despair, terror, and boredom of existence'.[2] It is not simply that as Lenz sees them, the earth, the wind, the water and so on are infused with a life of their own (although that is important too), but that there is something vaster, more embracing, more uplifting, there too, something on the order of the Cosmos, and it is this that he longs to be a part of. Lenz 'thought he should draw the storm right into himself, embrace all things within his being, he spread and lay over the entire earth, he burrowed his way into the All, it was an ecstasy that hurt; or else he stopped and laid his head in the moss and half closed his eyes, then everything receded far away, the earth beneath him shrank'.[3] In other words, the fact that he sees flowers respiring with the moon's nocturnal cycle is one sign among several of Lenz's altered state of mind. He is preoccupied with machines.

> Everything is a machine. Celestial Machines, the stars or rainbows in the sky, alpine machines – all of them connected to those of his body. The continual whirr of machines. '[Lenz] thought that it must be a feeling of endless bliss to be in contact with the profound life of every form, to have a soul for rocks, metals, water, and plants, to take himself, as into a dream, every element of nature, like flowers that breathe with the waxing and waning of the moon.' To be a chlorophyll- or a photosynthesis-machine, or at least slip his body into such machines as one part among the others. (AO, 2/8)

It is this preoccupation with machines that is the surest sign of the presence of the disease. Each of these machines, each of these possible states of being, is a zone of intensity that Lenz passes through. Lenz is *Homo natura* because he feels he is at one with the production of nature, but he is *Homo historia* inasmuch as he registers that production of nature as though it were somebody other than himself who was witnessing it. His ego is evacuated from its position in the centre of his sense of subject-hood. It can be said, to paraphrase Deleuze and Guattari, that there is no Lenz-the-self, author of dramatic works, who suddenly loses his mind and supposedly identifies with all sorts of strange states of being (blissful contact with rocks, metals, plants, and so on); rather, there is the Lenzian subject who passes through a series of states, and who identifies these states with the elements of nature as so many names from history (there is in this regard little difference between saying 'I am a rock' and 'I am Attila the Hun').

Following Pierre Klossowski's account of Nietzsche's fall into madness, Deleuze and Guattari argue that schizo subject is produced – produces itself in other words – as a residiuum or spare part that sits alongside the desiring-machine, which by virtue of the disease process now occupies centre stage. The states of intensity – e.g., his feeling for the 'soul' of rocks and so forth – through which the subject passes in its bid to relocate its centre form concentric circles around the desiring-machine. The subject passes through the specific band of intensity of one circle and then passes on to the next circle, like so many circles of hell. He is at one with the rocks, then water, then plants, and so on. As Klossowski puts it:

> The centrifugal forces do not flee the centre forever, but approach it once again, only to retreat from it yet again: such is the nature of the violent oscillations that overwhelm an individual so long as he seeks only his own centre and is incapable of seeing the circle of which he himself is a part; for if these oscillations overwhelm him, it is because each one of them corresponds to an individual other than the one he believes himself to be, from the point of view of the unlocatable centre. As a result, an identity is essentially fortuitous, and a series of individualities must be undergone by each of these oscillations, so that as a consequence the fortuitousness of this or that particular individuality will render all of them necessary. (cited in AO, 22/27–8)

Hence Lenz's desire to burrow into the All, to find the place where the radiating circles originate, the place he supposes must be calm, the zero degree of intensity.

The point that needs to be emphasized here is that if Lenz was not schizophrenic, if he wasn't in the grip of a schizophrenic episode, his walk through the mountains would have had a completely different texture. Doubtless it would lack the intensity of feeling apparent in Büchner's beautiful evocation of the troubled writer's mental life. The flowers would just be flowers, the earth merely dirt under foot, which is why Deleuze and Guattari insist on schizophrenia's inherent creativity, its productivity.[4] Everything is a machine to Lenz *because* he is a schizophrenic. The celestial machines, the alpine machine, the chlorophyll-machine and the photosynthesis-machine he perceives all around him or somehow feels are at work within him are all manifestations of the disease process. The same must be said of the eccentricities of Schreber and Malone and the many other equally strange characters whose stories are threaded throughout the pages of *Anti-Oedipus*. Deleuze and Guattari do not say schizophrenia is everywhere; rather what they say is that desiring-production is everywhere, but it is only visible to us in its raw state in schizophrenic delirium. Desiring-production is their neologism for a conception of desire infused with production – the first of their two strategic goals.

Deleuze and Guattari will later qualify their definition of desiring-production in a very important way that will help put the first chapter in perspective. Desiring-production is that aspect of the operation of the unconscious that cannot be assimilated by what they refer to as social production and reproduction, or more simply as the socius (AO, 189/204). As we'll see in what follows, desiring-production is that aspect of desire that the body without organs as the agent of anti-production is unable to contain, unable to force onto its smooth surface and thereby repress it (the Body without Organs is in fact defined by Deleuze and Guattari as the site of primary repression [AO, 10/15]). Larry Clark's short film 'Impaled', which was his contribution to the collective project entitled *Destricted*, offers an excellent, albeit rather graphic, illustration of what is meant here. The film begins with a series of interviews with young men who have answered an advertisement looking for people interested in working in pornographic films, but who haven't yet had any actual experience in that profession. From the short list of guys one is chosen and he then interviews several women who are professional pornographic movie performers. He then chooses one that he would most like to have sex with and they duly do a 'scene' together. What makes this film interesting for our purposes here is that the camera doesn't stop running between takes, not even when there is the need to clean up after a messy attempt at anal sex. In these moments, which would not normally be included in a pornographic film, we suddenly realize that contrary to popular perception pornography does not 'show it all' (as Žižek puts it[5]), but only displays that which can be coded as belonging to the domain of the 'sexual'. This domain, at least insofar as pornography is concerned, does not include the necessary interruptions to the performance of the sexual act that filming requires – such as the need to move the camera, alter lighting, revive a flagging male star, and so on. The distinction between eroticism and pornography is in this sense more apparent than real because neither 'show it all'. Both modes have at the core an element of anti-production, a body without organs, selecting what can and cannot be shown. Showing all really means showing that which eludes or estranges (in Brecht's sense) erotic overcoding and this is precisely what Larry Clark's film does.

It is in this sense, then, that Deleuze and Guattari define the schizophrenic as the limit of the socius, the instance of a pure asociality which terrifies every social organization. The schizophrenic is the living instance of the socially unassimilable being, or what Hardt and Negri refer to as the 'new barbarian' (the body incapable of obe-dience or submission).[6] Desiring-production is that aspect of desire which if it were to pass into social production and reproduction would sow the seeds of disorder and revolution as it does every time a little piece of it manages to elude the coding society imposes on it so as to contain it. That is why we only see desiring-production in its pure state in pathological cases, it only shows up where the appara-tuses of the social machinery have ceased to function. At length, then, we can say this is why the schizo going for a stroll is a better model than the neurotic on the couch – it reveals the schizophrenic process and in doing so tells us something essential about the way the unconscious works. But this picture of the schizophrenic as *Homo natura* and *Homo historia* is far from a complete account of Deleuze and Guattari's analysis of the schizophrenic process.

The traditional logic of desire is all wrong

There is still a step to be made between this account of the schizo-phrenic process as it operates in known cases of schizophrenia and the third aim of the case analyses under discussion here, namely the claim that this process is the basic matrix of the unconscious. As I mentioned above, Deleuze and Guattari are of the view that the schizophrenic deliriums they discuss could not take the forms they do if desiring-production, the motive force behind all delirium, did not work the way they say it does. In other words, they arrive at their understanding of desiring-production via a process of deduction. Like a pair of detectives they ask, 'Given a certain effect, what machine is capable of producing it? And given a machine, what can it be used for?' (AO, 3/8).

Can we possibly guess, for instance, what a knife rest is used for if all we are given is a geometrical description of it? Or yet another example: on being confronted with a complete machine made up of six stones in the right-hand pocket of my coat (the pocket that serves as the source of the stones), five stones in the right-hand pocket of my trousers, and five in my left-hand pocket (transmission pockets), with the remaining pocket of my coat receiving the stones that have already been handled, as each of the stones moves forward one pocket, how can we determine the effect of this circuit of distribution in which the mouth, too, plays a role as a stone-sucking machine? Where in this entire circuit do we find the production of sexual pleasure? (AO, 3/8)

It is the final question – where do we find the production of sexual pleasure? – which is the most telling, because what it points to is an essential difference between psychoanalysis and schizoanalysis at the level of their respective starting premises. Psychoanalysis assumes that all behaviour which isn't manifestly sexual, but isn't obviously ordinary or mundane either (i.e., nonsexual), must somehow be a substitute for sex, a perversion in other words. This is where Deleuze and Guattari part ways with Freud.

> We have difficulty understanding what principles psychoanalysis uses to support its conception of desire, when it maintains that the libido must be desexualised or even sublimated in order to proceed to the social investments, and inversely that the libido only resexualises these investments during the course of pathological regression. (AO, 322/348)

The problem here is twofold: psychoanalysis cannot account for 'the satisfaction the handyman [bricoleur] experiences when he plugs something into an electrical socket' (AO, 8/13) except in sexual terms, which it rules out; nor can it see the sexuality evident in the peculiar pleasure the bureaucrat takes in creating a well-ordered universe of files and reports, spreadsheets and databases, that he creates for himself, except as a perversion. Could we not say the same thing of countless other routine or mundane activities with which we fill our days? What is the pleasure of sitting on a beach on a hot day? Is it the hot white sand between our toes, the stinging sweat in our eyes, the burning sun on our back or the cool blue water before us beckoning us to explore its mysterious depths? What keeps us going back to the beach day after day, year after year? Maybe it's the combined voyeuristic and exhibitionistic thrill of being able to look at and be seen by other semi-clad people – the browned, the reddened, and the glistening, oily, sandy bodies, spread-eagled in the sand like so many chimeras. But if so, why not stay at home in the air-conditioning and watch a porno or re-runs of *Baywatch*? What specifically is it about the beach that draws us there so compellingly? By the same token, why doesn't everyone feel the same way? How can another loathe what I love? The pleasure of the beach has indeed been described in terms of transgression and the violating of taboos – but despite the resonances such analyses are able to generate, ultimately they fail to answer one basic question: why the beach? Doubtless the analyses of transgression are true on one level, but the symbolic overcoding it relies on tells us nothing about the simpler pleasure 'insisting' beneath these conscious thrills in the unconscious and the preconscious – the feel of the sand, the sun, the water. This 'insistence' of desire is ultimately what Deleuze and Guattari are trying to account for with the concept of the desiring-machine. We could of course spin out countless other examples and questions.

> The truth is that sexuality is everywhere: the way a bureaucrat fondles his records, a judge administers justice, a businessman causes money to circulate; the way the bourgeoisie fucks the proletariat; and so on. And there is no need to resort to metaphors, any more than for the libido to go by way of metamorphoses. Hitler got the fascists sexually aroused. Flags, nations, armies, banks get a lot of people aroused. (AO, 322/348)

The shift in perspective palpable here is more far-reaching than meets the eye. It necessitates a complete change in how desire is conceptualized, not just by psychoanalysis, but virtually the whole of the Western philosophical tradition to this point. Deleuze and Guattari repolarize it around an affirmative notion of production, setting aside the standard negative notion of desire as lack or need. On Deleuze and Guattari's view of things, desire does not need to be stimulated by an exogenous force such as need or want, it is a stimulus in its own right. This brings us to the key proposition advanced by this chapter, which as we'll see in more detail in the discussion of the fourth chapter of *Anti-Oedipus* is in fact one of the four principal theses of schizoanalysis: Deleuze and Guattari propose that *every investment of desire is social.*

> We maintain that the social field is immediately invested by desire, that it is the historically determined product of desire, and that libido has no need of any mediation or sublimation, any psychic operation, any transformation, in order to invade and invest the productive forces and the relations of production. *There is only desire and the social, and nothing else.* (AO, 31/36 emphasis in original)

They mean this to be understood in two ways. First, against the orthodoxy of psychoanalysis, it means desire invests the social field directly and without need of the mediation of fantasy (power doesn't excite us because it reminds us of our father, but because it resonates with the productivity of the unconscious itself). Second, against the orthodoxy of Marxism, it means that desire has no need of the deceptions of ideology in order to invest the social. We'll examine these points in more detail in the discussion of chapter two, but suffice it to say for now that Deleuze and Guattari's theory of desire implies a model of the unconscious which exerts far greater influence on the subject, yet also has far more psychical independence than either psychoanalysis or Marxism allow for. This isn't to say that they don't consider either the actuality or possibility of either psychic repression or social repression because in fact they do – indeed, one must say repression plays a far greater role in their work than their liberatory rhetoric would seem to allow.

> To a certain degree the traditional logic of desire is all wrong from the outset: from the very first step that the Platonic logic of desire forces us to take, making us choose between *production* and *acquisition*. From the moment we place desire on the side of the acquisition, we make desire an idealistic (dialectical, nihilistic) conception, which causes us to look upon it primarily as a lack: a lack of an object, a lack of the real object. (AO, 26/32)

The other path, the path of 'production', makes desire a process, something we do. By making desire lack we effectively subordinate it to another process, namely need, and make that its support, because if we only desire what we lack then we would still have to explain how it came to be that we were lacking that thing. Obviously, in doing so, we sacrifice the process of desire *qua* desire and turn it into a second-order concept. By contrast, Deleuze and Guattari argue that desire isn't 'bolstered by needs, but rather the contrary; needs are derived from desire: they are counterproducts within the real that desire produces.' (AO, 28/34). It is true the path of 'production' hasn't been completely ignored by philosophy. They credit Kant's *Critique of Judgement* with inaugurating something of 'a critical revolution as regards the theory of desire' (AO, 26–7/32). But, they add, it is no coincidence that Kant illustrates this definition of desire with fancies, hallucinations and delusions. In other words, for Kant the power of the mind to produce its own object means that the

> reality of the object, insofar as it is produced by desire, is thus a *psychic reality*. Hence it can be said that Kant's critical revolution changes nothing essential: this way of conceiving of productivity does not question the validity of the classical conception of desire as a lack; rather, it uses this conception as a support and a buttress, and merely examines it more carefully. (AO, 27/32)

Following the same logic, Deleuze and Guattari go on to say that desire conceived as the production of fantasies, which is the imagined compensation and substitute for the real object has 'been explained perfectly by psychoanalysis' (AO, 27/33). But, they imply, psychoanalysis has totally misunderstood desire's actual function, which is not at all the production of fantasies, which is merely a secondary operation, but the production of production itself.

> There is no such thing as the social production of reality on the one hand, and a desiring-production that is mere fantasy on the other. The only connections that could be established between these two productions would be the secondary ones of introjection and projection, as though all social practices had their precise counterpart in introjected or internal mental practices, or as though mental practices were projected upon social systems, without either of the two sets of practices ever having any real or concrete effect upon the other. (AO, 30/36)

Thus we return to the problem of desiring-production. It is true, as I'll discuss more fully below, desiring-production cannot operate without simultaneously producing new desiring-machines and destroying old desiring-machines, but that doesn't mean they are desiring-production and desiring-machines indistinguishable from each other as in the proverbial case of the night when all cows are black. They are both an essential part of what Deleuze and Guattari refer to as the *process* of desire, each with quite different roles to play. As I've said, *Anti-Oedipus* opens with three purposely off-the-wall snapshots of desiring-machines in full flight, implying that these be given primacy, but in the true conceptual order of things it is in fact desiring-production that is the primary term. This point has to be insisted on because Deleuze and Guattari's rather delirious presentation of desiring-machines in their schizophrenic mode in these opening pages can have a blinkering effect: first of all, it makes it seem as though this is the *only* way desiring-machines can be formed, which is not the case (as Deleuze and Guattari themselves acknowledge there are also desiring-machines of a paranoid or perverted type too); second, and equally problematically, it makes it seem that desiring-machines of this type are in and of themselves desirable, which again is not the case (Deleuze and Guattari acknowledge that the schizophrenic in full flight is bereft of all the usual social ties and is therefore not the model of a revolutionary); and third, perhaps most insidiously of all, it obscures the relation between desiring-production and desiring-machines, which is by no means as straightforward as it initially appears (as we shall see, there are several modalities of desiring-production). So what is desiring-production? Putting it in psychoanalytic terms, it is the production of the Real in itself, or better yet it is the Real conceived as process rather than unreachable limit – it is not so much unrepresentable (Lacan's thesis) as non-representational (AO, 59/61). Putting it in schizoanalytic terms, the Real 'is the end product, the result of the passive syntheses of desire as the autoproduction of the unconscious' (AO, 28/34).

The passive syntheses of desire

The great discovery of psychoanalysis was that of the production of desire, of the productions of the unconscious. (AO, 25/31)

The productive unconscious – i.e., desire or desiring-production – is a synthesizing machine, a factory, but the syntheses it performs are neither all of the same type, nor all of the same order. Moreover it is double in character: it has both a *nature* and *regime*. Its nature is what it is capable of, what it can do, its competence if you will; while its regime is what it does when it is doing what it is capable of, its performance in other words. The productive unconscious, then, in all its guises as desire and desiring-production, terms Deleuze and Guattari use interchangeably, is 'the set of *passive syntheses* that engineer partial objects, flows, and bodies, and that function as units of production' (i.e., the desiring-machines and their objects) (AO, 28/34). As I will explain in more detail in what follows, the concept of passive synthesis and with it the schizoanalytic apparatus as a whole rests on the philosophical foundation Deleuze put in place in *Difference and Repetition*, particularly his magnificent conceptualization of the three syntheses of time: habit, memory and death.[7]

Passive synthesis combines three distinct kinds of operation, which taken together comprise the three modes of desire understood as a machine: (i) the synthesis of connection, (ii) the synthesis of disjunction, and (iii) the synthesis of conjunction. As I will discuss in more detail in relation to chapter 2, each of these three types of synthesis may go one of two ways, according to which type of *regime* is in ascendancy. *This variation in what may be termed the modality of the syntheses is the principle analytic mechanism constructed by Deleuze and Guattari to explain contemporary social and political behaviour and attitudes.* It is this mechanism which enables the notions of desiring-production and desiring-machines to be used for analytic purposes. My implication is that passive syntheses form the analytic backbone of *Anti-Oedipus* – they give rise to the basic concept of the desiring-machines as well as the means of establishing an effective connection between psychoanalysis and Marxism, or more particularly individual desire and social control. This mechanism is the principal subject of chapter 2 of *Anti-Oedipus*. Here, then, I will briefly explore the origin and derivation of the concept of passive synthesis as it was developed in Deleuze's work prior to his meeting with Guattari.

I will start with the big picture – the notion of passive synthesis itself – and then move onto the specifics of how its individual parts function. Essentially, what I want to establish to begin with is that although Deleuze and Guattari rarely use the term 'passive synthesis' apart from the one mention cited above (which probably explains why very few of their commentators have latched onto it), without it we cannot explain what desire is, we can only say what it does, and even then we are restricted to sheer description.[8] It is only with the concept of passive synthesis in place that desire becomes an analytic concept, a concept capable of generating concrete social and political critique. Contrary to Peter Hallward, who pays very little attention to the role of passive synthesis in Deleuze's work, in spite of his obsessive cavilling against the latter's 'constructivism', passive synthesis is perfectly able to account for 'cumulative transformation or novelty in terms of actual materials and tendencies'.[9] Indeed, I would go so far as to say that *it is only with the aid of the concept of passive synthesis* that one can accomplish this task without falling into the very idealism of which Hallward accuses Deleuze. Passive synthesis is Deleuze's means of solving the problem of constructing a genuine philosophy of immanence without at the same time losing his grip on the 'real world'.

The basic problem facing the philosophy of immanence is this: how can the mind constitute itself without first of all having an idea of itself?[10] The answer is that it cannot do so unless, as both the Kantian and Hegelian traditions do, it first of all posits a prior and necessarily higher category capable of comprehending it, such as the Mind or the Spirit. Deleuze's solution, which goes in the reverse direction to Kant and Hegel, is to posit at a foundational level a set of passive syntheses that are constitutive without being active. These syntheses have no self-comprehension of what they are doing, much less an end or goal – they simply act, as unthinkingly as machines.[11] There is a necessary circularity here: the syntheses produce everything, even themselves. Chaos, Deleuze's definition of nothingness, is the passive syntheses turning in a void, ceaselessly operating, but not producing anything.

In *Difference and Repetition*, Deleuze defines passive synthesis as follows: 'It is not carried out by the mind, but occurs *in* the mind which contemplates, prior to all memory and all reflection.' (DR, 71/97). This is the schizo process *avant la lettre*. This is desiring-production *avant la lettre*. As Deleuze and Guattari formulate it, then, the question 'how does desire work?' is effectively the same question as 'how does the unconscious come into being?' Both questions turn on essentially the same problem, namely the autoproduction of the Real. 'Following Condillac', Deleuze writes, 'we must regard habit as the foundation from which all other psychic phenomena derive.' (DR, 78/107). The passive synthesis of habit 'constitutes the habit of living, our expectation that "it" will continue'. (DR, 74/101). Habits are the 'presents' (moments of pure lived time) the imagination seizes from the flow of time, without ever ceasing to be temporal. Passive synthesis, then, is not just a capacity to receive sensation, as Kant might have it, but implies a synthetic ability to constitute the sensate organism as well.

There are two levels of habit, or what Deleuze also calls 'constituent passivity': organic synthesis and perceptual synthesis. In both cases, though, habit is used in a pre-subjective sense. It doesn't refer to the habits, good or bad, of a fully formed subject, like smoking, or reading the Sunday papers in bed. It is not something 'I' do. It belongs rather to the order of the formation of the organism itself, at its most elementary. The capacity to contract a habit is in this respect the most basic prerequisite of the organism. Habit is a mode of contraction. Contraction for Deleuze is the synthetic basis of all life forms, describing literally how they come into being. At the level of organic synthesis: 'We are made of contracted water, earth, light and air – not merely prior to recognition or representation of these, but prior to their being sensed. Every organism, in its receptive and perceptual elements, but also in its viscera, is a sum of contractions, of retentions and expectations.' (DR, 73/100). Contraction is contemplation, or rather it is what one does in contemplating – but we must not think the 'one' here implies a conscious human subject because even wheat can be considered a contraction of earth, air and soil. 'A soul must be attributed to the heart, to the muscles, nerves and cells, but a contemplative soul whose entire function is to contract a habit.' (DR, 74/101). Contraction is the dual process of selecting what is good and needful from the environment and setting aside everything else as either superfluous or poisonous. Perceptual synthesis works in exactly the same way and always in concert with organic synthesis as shown by von Uexküll's celebrated analysis of the tick, with its three affects: sensitivity to light, sense of smell, penetrating mouth (ATP, 283/314).

As Deleuze himself acknowledges, many people will not recognize the foregoing as belonging to the order of habit because there doesn't seem to be any action or activity in the processes related to contraction. This owes, he says, to a psychological illusion and a fetish for activity which misunderstands the very process of learning itself because it fails to grasp that contemplation is not the activity of a self, but the passive synthesis of what we mistake for a self. Deleuze rejects the *a priori* assumption that the self is an integrated global whole (the psychoanalytic theory of the fractured subject is in his view a complicated variant on this assumption). He takes the view, rather, that behind the façade of

> the self which acts are little selves which contemplate and which render possible both the action and the active subject. We speak of our 'self' only in virtue of these thousands of little witnesses which contemplate within us: it is always a third party who says 'me'. (DR, 75/103)

Although Deleuze often refers to these thousands of little witnesses as partial objects, they are neither the bereft fragments of a shattered unity nor the scattered pieces of an as yet unassembled puzzle.

Selves are larval subjects; the world of passive syntheses constitutes the system of the self, under conditions yet to be determined, but it is the system of a dissolved self. There is a self wherever a furtive contemplation has been established, whenever a contracting machine capable of drawing a difference from repetition functions somewhere. (DR, 78–9/107)

The contracting machine Deleuze speaks of here would in due course be rechristened 'desiring-production' and the larval selves it gives rise to 'desiring-machines'. In short, practically the entire theoretical apparatus underpinning *Anti-Oedipus* and subsequent volumes is worked out here in detail.

The three syntheses

The three passive syntheses are as follows:

1. Connective Synthesis – mobilizes the Libido as withdrawal energy (*énergie de prélèvement*)
2. Disjunctive Synthesis – mobilizes the Numen as detachment energy (*énergie de détachement*)
3. Conjunctive Synthesis – mobilizes Voluptas as residual energy (*énergie de résiduelle*)

Marx's general formula of capital (MCM') provides the underpinning model (or 'metamodel' as Guattari would term it) for these syntheses, both individually and in relation to each (AO, 4/9–10). This model describes the basic working of the unconscious as Deleuze and Guattari see it.

Giovanni Arrighi helpfully exfoliates Marx's famous formula as follows: 'Money capital (M) means liquidity, flexibility, freedom of choice. Commodity capital (C) means capital invested in a particular input-output combination in view of a profit. Hence it means concreteness, rigidity, and a narrowing down or closing of options. M' means *expanded* liquidity, flexibility, and freedom of choice.'[12] The crucial historical point here is that capitalists do not invest in 'particular input-output combinations' as an end in itself, but do so with a view to obtaining even greater flexibility of investment, and in times of trouble will always tend to retreat to a position of flexibility. More generally, what this means is that capitalists do not invest in relatively risky and inflexible investments such as manufacturing plants for the sake of it, but do so with a view to enhancing their base of capital so as to increase their overall liquidity and the flexibility that results.[13]

> Marx's general formula of capital (MCM') can therefore be interpreted as depicting not just the logic of individual capitalist investments, but also a recurrent pattern of historical capitalism as a world system. The central aspect of this pattern is the alternation of epochs of material expansion (MC phases of capital accumulation) with phases of financial rebirth and expansion (CM').[14]

In the first phase, money capital 'sets in motion' a vast range of activities, but centres principally on converting raw materials into finished commodities, and derives its impetus to growth from the sale of these manufactured objects. In the second phase, however, this money capital, having achieved a critical mass, basically 'sets itself free' from its dependency on objects and expands through exclusively financial deals in banking, insurance, derivatives, bond trading and lately the exploitation of intellectual property.

The three syntheses of desire correspond to the three phases in Marx's general formula of capital, namely MCM': the synthesis of connection is the 'free labour' or 'primitive accumulation' phase that sets everything in motion; the synthesis of disjunction corresponds to the intermediate phase of investment in industry (input-output combinations); and the synthesis of conjunction is the third phase in which money capital is set free all over again. This model is, however, very far from describing a steady-state system. It is subject to a law of declining rate of profit as the market reaches saturation point and capital itself attains such a bloated size it can no longer continue to expand at the same rate. This is the position of corporations like Microsoft who having attained not only a near monopoly in the software market but a virtual saturation of it as well (something like 98 per cent of all computers in the world use a Microsoft operating system) can no longer continue to grow by selling software to new customers; it must either diversify into new lines such as the internet and compete with the all-conquering Google, or cannibalize its own customer base by releasing new operating systems that are not back-compatible with the existing systems. But this really only refers to what Arrighi designates as the MC phase of capital accumulation. The second CM' phase can only be seen by stepping outside of the confines of Microsoft and looking at the software industry as a whole. The fact that it is reported in the business press that investors are growing nervous about Microsoft's capacity to lift itself out of its current crisis of accumulation suggests that capital is getting ready to take flight from this corporation and start looking for new ways of setting things in motion all over again (hence, no doubt, its merger talks with Yahoo). It could be that Microsoft is coming up against its own immanent limit, the point past which it cannot grow.

Viewed from the perspective of the software industry as a whole, it is clear that capital is following Marx's formula to the letter. Venture capital – the free flowing money that results from primitive accumulation – seeks out 'particular input-output combinations' in the form of dot.com start-ups in the expectation of being rapidly converted back into venture capital so the process can be resumed all over again elsewhere. As Marx himself emphasized, and Deleuze and Guattari reiterate, this process contains a double movement – on the one hand, it creates new investment opportunities by breaking with convention and entering new territory, which in the early 1990s the internet was (deterritorialization); but on the other hand, as these opportunities peter out and returns dwindle it falls back on tradition and resurrects images of the past in an attempt to maintain momentum (reterritorialization). This is precisely what is happening with the internet now: recent market trends suggest that the dot.com business has lately moved out of the MC phase and entered the terminal CM' phase. Although new internet business applications are springing up all the time, and the market is so far maintaining its faith in them, it is hard to avoid the glaring fact that the general tendency of these businesses is to follow old, established patterns of profit making. There is a distinct staleness in their thinking that their technological wizardry cannot disguise. After all, eBay is simply a global fleamarket and Amazon a global bazaar, business models which date back to ancient times.

New applications of technology are not matched by new ways of generating surplus value. For all its innovation in establishing the search-engine as a 'model of realization' (Deleuze and Guattari's term for what the financial press calls a 'business model'), it ultimately relies on the idea of paid advertising pioneered by newspapers in the nineteenth century. More striking still, the current Wunderkinder of the internet, Myspace and Youtube, are yet to realize a profit from their actual business activities – they are trading on their 'cultural' value, using our interest in the service they provide to counteract the real fact of their loss-making and render themselves valuable to other corporations. In this way, canny investors in these start-up corporations have been able to make a substantial profit from profitless ventures simply by selling them to larger media corporations (Google and Fox respectively), thus confirming the general point that in the third M' phase money simply begets money without the necessity of a mediation through commodity production. In other words, the limit Microsoft faces is not the same as the one capital as a whole faces – it can always move on. By deserting unprofitable investments in favour of lucrative opportunities elsewhere, capital itself thrives even when individual companies – even giant companies like Microsoft – do not.[15]

The unconscious as Deleuze and Guattari conceive it is subject to these same laws, these same processes, these same cyclical turns in production. To begin with, there is the synthesis of connection, also known as 'the production of production', which sets everything in motion by coupling continuous flows of libido with partial objects that interrupt the flow and draw sustenance from it. 'Desire causes the current to flow, itself flows in turn, and breaks the flow.' (AO, 6/11). The assemblage of milk-producing breast and the suckling-mouth is Deleuze and Guattari's standard image for this process, but it is a deceptive image because it obfuscates the fact that the synthesis of connection is an abstract process which can be found literally everywhere. In spite of the emphasis Deleuze and Guattari give to bodily functions and bodily fluids – shitting, fucking, etc. – we will never understand the concept of synthesis unless we realize that it is fundamentally virtual in nature. The same must be said for desiring-machines – the breast and mouth may be the component parts of a particular desiring-machine, but it is the relationship between them that is machinic not the respective body parts.

Even though the synthesis of connection refers to actual connections between real flows and real objects, actual breasts and actual mouths, it isn't itself actual. Though fully real, its mode of being is entirely virtual. For our purposes, it is entrepreneurial capitalism that gives us the best sense of how the synthesis of connection (along with the parallel syntheses of disjunction and conjunction), works in real terms. As I mentioned above, the synthesis of connection corresponds to what Marx referred to as 'primitive accumulation', the process whereby money and commodities are transformed into capital. This can only occur under special conditions, Marx says, namely the moment when two very different types of commodity owners – the owners of the means of production and the owners of labour, the so-called 'free' workers who are neither part of the means of production (as slaves would be), nor owners of the means of production (as self-employed peasant proprietors would be) – meet and form a productive relationship. 'So-called primitive accumulation, therefore, is nothing else than the historical process of divorcing the producer ["free" labour] from the means of production. It appears as "primitive" because it forms the pre-history of capital, and of the mode of production corresponding to capital.'[16] This history, Marx adds, 'is written in the annals of mankind in letters of blood and fire'.[17]

Synthesis of connection

The synthesis of connection is the process whereby desire exploits the body to its own ends. In this scenario, desire is the equivalent of capital: it owns the means of production, but lacks the labourers needed to realize its potential. In order to obtain the labour it needed to staff its mines, factories, agribusinesses, and so forth, capital had to first of all 'free' it from the various social bonds of the soil and the guild and thereby transform peasants and journeymen into wage-labourers. As Marx notes, to the bourgeois historian this process appears emancipatory, but this is only true to the extent that we also observe that these workers were simultaneously 'robbed of all their own means of production, and all the guarantees of existence afforded by the old feudal arrangements'.[18] Following Lacan, but clearly in sympathy with Marx, Deleuze and Guattari refer to this process of desire as the *procurement phase*: desire follows the same path as primitive accumulation, it first of all disjoints the body into its component organs (i.e., it breaks up the feudal arrangements tying labour to the land or the guild) and then sheers these parts from their own powers (i.e., it alienates their labour) (AO, 44/49). As Marx puts it, capital pays for the power of individual labourers, but not their combined power.[19] Having taken control of the organs it then reorganizes them to suit its needs – thus the labourer's muscle power is harnessed to the machine, and its movements subordinated to its rhythm.

This is what Deleuze and Guattari mean when they say the desiring-machines try to make us into organisms – the synthesis of connection snaps our organs together in a new arrangement of its own making and its own design. On this view of things, organs are any parts of the body which seen from the perspective of the unconscious are capable of performing labour, capable in other words of producing a flow themselves, but also of turning the ceaseless flow of libido into an affect (i.e., 'cathexis' in Freud's terms), that is to say both an interruption and conversion of desire. These parts, the organs, are the equivalent of free labour inasmuch as their productivity is henceforth in the service of another party, namely capital itself. This labour is productive in Marx's sense because it advances the objectives of capital itself by producing surplus value. This is why Deleuze and Guattari say that producing is always something 'grafted onto' the object, namely the organs (AO, 6/12). The essential point here is that primitive accumulation gives rise to something greater than itself: not merely capital, but the capitalist class itself, henceforth the new rulers of the earth.

> This is the body that Marx is referring to when he says that it is not the product of labour, but rather appears as its natural or divine presupposition. In fact, it does not restrict itself merely to opposing productive forces in and of themselves. It falls back on (*il se rabat sur*) all production, constituting a surface over which the forces and agents of production are distributed, thereby appropriating for itself all surplus production and arrogating to itself both the whole and the parts of the process, which now seem to emanate from it as a quasi cause. Forces and agents come to represent a miraculous form of its own power: they appear 'miraculated' (*miraculés*) by it. (AO, 11/16)

This brings us to the second synthesis, the synthesis of disjunction, or separation phase.

Synthesis of disjunction
The synthesis of disjunction operates on the platform created by primitive accumulation, which Deleuze and Guattari refer to as the body without organs. Its basic model is that of the binary distinction – rich and poor, brave and cowardly, straight and gay, and so on. Its energy, which Deleuze and Guattari define as divine, comes

from its connection to the body without organs, which might usefully be regarded as its dialectical complement.

> The body without organs is produced as a whole, but in its own particular place within the process of production, alongside the parts that it neither unifies nor totalises. And when it operates on them, when it turns back upon them (*se rabat sur elles*), it brings about transverse communications, transfinite summarisations, polyvocal and transcursive inscriptions on its own surface, on which the functional breaks of partial objects are continually intersected by breaks in signifying chains, and by breaks effected by a subject that uses them as reference points in order to locate itself. The whole not only coexists with all the parts; it is contiguous to them, it exists as a product that is produced apart from them and yet at the same time is related to them. (AO, 47/51–2)

Translating this back into economic theory, what Deleuze and Guattari are effectively saying is that the process of primitive accumulation produces as a by-product something not only greater than itself, but something that ultimately triumphs over it, arrogating to itself all of the latter's productive power. As Marx argued, capital soaks up the productive power of its workers and represents it back to them as its own power. 'On entering the labour process' the so-called free workers (i.e., the syntheses of connection)

> are incorporated into capital [i.e., the body without organs]. As co-operators, as members of a working organism, they merely form a particular mode of existence of capital. Hence the productive power developed by the worker socially is the productive power of capital. The socially productive power of labour develops as a free gift to capital whenever the workers are placed under certain conditions, and it is capital which places them under these conditions. Because this power costs capital nothing, while on the other hand it is not developed by the worker until his labour itself belongs to capital, it appears as a power which capital possesses by its nature – a productive power inherent in capital.[20]

The term 'the body without organs' is borrowed from Antonin Artaud, but it is in vain that we look to his work for an explanation of what Deleuze and Guattari have in mind. Marx is a far better guide. The synthesis of disjunction corresponds to the C phase when capital (body without organs) invests directly in 'input-output combinations' (desiring-machines). As Arrighi indicates above, this phase is marked by a tension. The aim of capital is to increase its liquidity, to do this it risks investing in fixed situations, but the minute these investments perform contrary to expectations it retreats to its preferred liquid form. In Deleuze and Guattari's work this dualism is rewritten as the attraction/repulsion relation between the body without organs (capital in its liquid state) and the desiring-machines (capital in its invested and bound state). The synthesis of disjunction is in effect the genealogy of desire, or rather 'the form that the genealogy of desire assumes' (AO, 15/20).

The syntheses of disjunction are the means whereby the 'subject' differentiates itself from sheer matter and indeed from the smooth surface of the body without organs on which it stands. It takes the form of an 'either/or' judgement: am I parent or child? alive or dead? man or woman? (the neurotic's three questions, according to Lacan). But perhaps we could put it another way, more in keeping with the economic model we have been following. The essential question of the capitalist is always 'will it make a profit or not?' In other words, it is not simply a matter of deciding between being a parent or child, alive or dead, or even man or woman, but of determining the surplus value that will accrue to me for deciding correctly. It is in this sense functionally equivalent to the Althusserian concept of 'interpellation', with the body without organs standing in the place of ideology. For what do the ideological state apparatuses (i.e., social-machines) do but call on us to *reproduce the relations of production?*[21]

> The disjunctive synthesis of recording therefore comes to overlap the connective syntheses of production. The process as process of production extends into the method as method of inscription. Or rather, if what we term libido is the connective 'labour' of desiring-production, it should be said that part of this energy is transformed into the energy of disjunctive inscription (Numen). (AO, 14/19)

Undoubtedly, it is Althusser who has given us the best description of this state of affairs.

> As St Paul admirably put it, it is in the 'Logos', meaning in ideology [i.e., the body without organs], that we 'live, move and have our

being'. It follows that, for you and for me, the category of the subject is a primary 'obviousness' (obviousnesses are always primary): it is clear that you and I are subjects (free, ethical, etc. . . .). Like all obviousnesses, including those that make a word 'name a thing' or 'have a meaning' (therefore including the obviousness of the 'transparency' of language), the 'obviousness' that you and I are subjects – and that that does not cause any problems – is an ideological effect, the elementary ideological effect. It is indeed a peculiarity of ideology that it imposes (without appearing to do so, since these are 'obviousnesses') obviousnesses as obviousnesses, which we cannot *fail to recognise* and before which we have the inevitable and natural reaction of crying out (aloud or in the 'still, small voice of conscience'): 'That's obvious! That's right! That's true!'[22]

It is *this* effect – the creation and occupation of what we might term the plane or power of obviousness – that Deleuze and Guattari have in mind when they say given a certain effect we should inquire what machine is capable of producing it (AO, 3/8).

The true ideological power of capital is that it is able to portray itself, and not the sweat of labour that enabled it to come into being in the first place, as the real enabling force in contemporary society. Nowhere is this reversal of the actual order of things more starkly expressed than in the egregious neo-liberal idea of the 'trickle-down effect', which alleges that promoting 'big business' by giving it generous tax breaks or indeed 'tax holidays' is good for society as a whole because when 'big business' succeeds its prosperity must inevitably be distributed downwards in the form of increased consumer spending on the part of the rich. The same logic applies in Nobel Prize winner Hernando de Soto's bootstrapping model of economic development (expounded in the aptly named *The Mystery of Capital*), which proposes that the Third World can raise itself out of its poverty if it simply lowers the barriers to the wonderworking properties of capital by giving slum dwellers two things: land titles and access to micro credit. The trouble is, de Soto's policy ideas do not work for the general good of all, but in Mike Davis's memorable phrase 'simply grease the skids to a Hobbesian hell'.[23]

In practice, land titling in the slums leads to the creation of a slum-dwelling *rentier* class who use their freely acquired title to extort rent from the ceaseless influx of new residents who by virtue of the historical accident of arriving too late to receive the benefit of state's munificence must make do with what the market offers. In other words, land titling 'accelerates social differentiation in the slum and does nothing to aid renters, the actual majority of the poor in many cities'.[24] In turn, the newly created landholding class act as bankers to the renting class, thus acerbating an already desperate situation. The point is that there is nothing mysterious about capital, except the fact that as a society we tolerate its invidious effects. The body without organs, then, is simply not capital, but the acceptance of it as a model of right in Hegel's sense. Social differentiation, which presupposes the existence of capital, is indeed a perfect example of the synthesis of disjunction at work. This synthesis, which Deleuze and Guattari also refer to as a synthesis of recording, does not operate in the same way as the synthesis of connection; it expresses a law of distribution or inscription rather than combination or production. Its law is the law of what Žižek usefully calls the 'forced choice'.[25] For instance, de Soto tells the impoverished slum-dwellers that capitalism isn't the cause of their problems, but the cure. His message is clear: choose capitalism and you will be saved, not because it is the best available choice of economic models, but rather because *there is no other choice*. Slums exist, according to this viewpoint, because capital's principal mechanisms, private property and credit money, have been forestalled by short sighted policy making on the part of the state. But it is an easy and cheap fix – the state can use its power to legislate title into being and effectively grant slum-dwellers their property and then sit back and let the market take care of the rest. Either we acknowledge that capital is the only true economic model, or we condemn ourselves to a permanent state of poverty. The only way to break this deadlock, Deleuze and Guattari insist, is by jettisoning both the problem and the solution.

Synthesis of conjunction

Acceding to capitalism as a form of right has its rewards. Even in the slums, among the very poor, there are those who benefit from capital, however meagrely.

> Just as a part of the libido as energy of production was transformed into energy of recording (Numen), a part of this energy of recording is transformed into energy of consummation (Voluptas).

It is this residual energy that is the motive force behind the third synthesis of the unconscious: the conjunctive synthesis 'so it's . . .', or the production of consumption. (AO, 18/23)

The synthesis of conjunction takes place under the aegis of the previous two syntheses; it is the reward that falls to 'us' for assenting to an interpellation by the desiring-machines (all while forgetting that a choice was involved). Its model is clearly that of 'misrecognition', which as Althusser put it 'is of particular concern for all investigations into ideology'.[26] But whereas Althusser effectively conflates misrecognition with ideology, Deleuze and Guattari treat it as a product of the interaction between the body without organs and the desiring-machines. The subject suffers from the tension between the two states of desire – free and fixed – produced by the syntheses of connection and disjunction and unconsciously tries to reconcile this tension through the production of still another kind of machine, which the generic name 'celibate machine' may provisionally designate.

This is tantamount to saying that the subject is produced as a mere residuum alongside the desiring-machines, or that he confuses himself with this third productive machine and with the residual reconciliation that it brings about: a conjunctive synthesis of consummation in the form of a wonderstruck 'So *that's* what it was!' (AO, 19/23)

This tension is the basis of Deleuze and Guattari's explanation of what in Freud would be termed symptom formation.

PSYCHOANALYSIS AND FAMILIALISM: THE HOLY FAMILY

Given the syntheses of the unconscious, the practical problem is that of their use, legitimate or not, and of the conditions that define a use of synthesis as legitimate or not.

Gilles Deleuze and Félix Guattari, *Anti-Oedipus*

If I were to try to represent chapter 2 of *Anti-Oedipus* pictorially, I'd have to resort to one of those *trompe l'oeil* pictures of the type which depending on how you look at them show either a duck or rabbit, a wineglass or two people kissing, and so on, because it is effectively two chapters morphed into one. On the one hand there is a lengthy critique of the paralogisms of psychoanalysis *and* on the other hand there is the further elaboration of what I described with regard to the previous chapter as the *analytic mechanism* of schizo-analysis. Most readings of *Anti-Oedipus* emphasize the former, often at the expense of the latter. My approach will be more even-handed, but having said that my argument throughout is that to read *Anti-Oedipus* effectively we need to focus on the analytic mechanism it develops.

The fact is, Deleuze and Guattari do not reject psychoanalysis. This is a common misperception they themselves are largely respon-sible for. Contrary to popular myth, they explicitly state that they 'refuse to play "take it or leave it"' games with psychoanalysis and accept the edict that 'one cannot challenge the process of the "cure" except by starting from elements drawn from this cure.'[27] (AO, 128/140). In practice, they actually retain a number of psychoana-lytic concepts (such as primary and secondary repression, the ego, the drives, as well as the concept of the unconscious itself as a dis-tinct system within a system that also includes a preconscious and a conscious) and use them with only minimal retooling. Their stated aim is to engender what they term an 'internal reversal' in psycho-analysis and transform its 'analytic machine into an indispensable part of the revolutionary machinery' (AO, 90/97). The surprisingly Maoist implication of this aim is that social change can only be achieved via a 'cultural revolution', that is to say a revolution in the way people think rather than a revolution of arms. In other words, the critique of psychoanalysis advances the cause of schizoanalysis, but it is very far from being the main purpose of either this chapter or the book as a whole.

The five paralogisms of psychoanalysis

As we read Deleuze and Guattari's critique of psychoanalysis, the question we need to keep uppermost in our minds is how do they propose to bring about the 'internal reversal' that will transform it into an indispensable component of a revolutionary programme? This goal, rather than the desire to refute psychoanalysis *tout court*, governs their approach to the work of Freud and his successors. Deleuze and Guattari identify five paralogisms (that is to say, five points of argument which are unintentionally or unknowingly invalid or false) in the *practice* of psychoanalysis. The paralogisms of:

1. extrapolation;
2. double bind;
3. application;
4. fictitious desire;
5. desiring-production.

The first three paralogisms are enumerated in the course of the explanation of the three passive syntheses and are in that sense corollaries of the respective syntheses. The fourth paralogism, arguably the most important of them all, provides a partial or pre-liminary explanation of how Oedipalization takes hold of the unconscious. The fifth paralogism brings us back full circle to where we began, namely the idea that desiring-production as an affirmative process defines the operation of the unconscious, not lack. What in all this the promised mechanism of 'internal reversal'? The short answer is the family. As will be seen below in the discussion of the individual paralogisms, Deleuze and Guattari reject psychoanaly-sis's apprehension of the family and propose four counter-theses:

1. the family is not the primary object of desire;
2. the family is the agent not the cause of psychic repression;
3. the family is an inductor not an organizer;
4. the family is the origin of the state's hold over us.

The family functions as a selection or triangulation of the subject. It identifies who belongs by right and who does not (AO, 114/124). It apportions roles which make us 'whole' persons – mum, dad, you, your brother and your sister, and so on. It determines what it is right and proper to do within the family – it instils the idea of the author-ity of the parent, the need to share and be fair among the siblings, and so on.[28] Once those selections have been made, once roles have been assigned and the good and bad objects decided, the family makes them all resonate together by connecting desire to these 'ready-mades' of social production. Ultimately, what Deleuze and Guattari propose as an 'internally reversed' form of psychoanalysis is one shorn of the family as the central organizing category. As Deleuze and Guattari conceive it, the family is not a microcosmic world within a world in which the drama of everyday life is played out in small form and in such a way as to render redundant that larger drama. It doesn't anticipate all the anxieties of later life by giving anxiety itself its first and as it were final form. Neither does it stamp our unconscious so that every event cannot but reverberate with the sound of its petty furies. The various elements of the family are constantly in touch with and connected to the 'elements of the political and historical situation' itself, which exceeds the reaches of Oedipus on all sides (AO, 107/115). Combining these points, Deleuze and Guattari formulate the rule:

> [T]he mother and the father exist only as fragments, and are never organised into a figure or a structure able both to represent the unconscious, and to represent in it the various agents of collectivity; rather, they always shatter into fragments that come into contact with these agents, meet them face to face, square off with them, or settle the differences with them as in hand-to-hand combat. (AO, 106–7/115)

We'll see below how this position is arrived at in the course of the enumeration of the five paralogisms.

The first paralogism of psychoanalysis, the paralogism of extrapolation, is this: psychoanalysis converts a detachable partial object – e.g., the penis – into a detached complete object, namely the phallus, from which all subjects then derive by power of its attribution of lack.[29] The phallus is the one thing both sexes have in common because they both suffer from its lack, albeit in different ways – for women it is their point of departure (what they desire, or envy, above all because they lack it), whereas for men it is effectively their destination (what they fear losing, above all, even though in a sense they've never had it since the phallus *qua* phallus is by definition an impossible, mythic object) (AO, 67/70). 'It is this conversion that makes the whole of sexuality shift into the Oedipal framework: this projection of all the break-flows onto the same mythical locale, and all the nonsignifying signs into the same major signifier.' (AO, 81–2/87).

By isolating the penis, which in Deleuze and Guattari's scheme of things is simply one potential desiring-machine among others, one possible partial object among many, and elevating it to the position of the One-All (to adapt the term Badiou misapplies to Deleuze's ontology[30]), i.e., the One that encompasses and includes under its auspices the All, the phallus loses its 'virulence and efficacy' and becomes instead a serene order of judgement, castrating everyone who falls under its gaze. The psychoanalytic 'cure', then, consists in teaching girls to renounce their envious desire for a penis and boys to renounce their 'protest', their apprehension that a 'passive' attitude towards other men amounts to the loss of their penis.[31] In this sense, it is psychoanalysis itself which is castrating: 'cured' is castrated (AO, 68/71). 'Here we have a properly analytical fallacy,' Deleuze and Guattari write,

> that consists in passing from the detachable object to the position of a complete object as the thing detached (phallus). This passage implies a subject, defined as a fixed ego of one sex or the other, who necessarily experiences as a lack his subordination to the tyrannical complete object. (AO, 68/71)

The fallacy consists in giving primacy to the symbolic object, i.e., the phallus, and consigning the actual penis and indeed all the sexual organs to the pre-oedipal realm, implying that desire is motivated by lack not plenitude.

This brings us to the second paralogism, the paralogism of the 'double bind'. Contrary to Gregory Bateson, who argues in *Steps to an Ecology of Mind* (the same book, incidentally, from which Deleuze and Guattari draw inspiration for the concept of 'plateau') that the family is schizophrenizing because of the impossible mutually exclusive demands it places on desire – love your parents, but not too much – Deleuze and Guattari argue that the family is Oedipalizing. More particularly, Deleuze and Guattari argue that the cure, rather than the disease, is the *double bind* (AO, 88/94). If one does not resign oneself to the fate of castration, and embrace the dictates of one's sex, then one is condemned to the proverbial dark night of the undifferentiated, the so-called 'polymorphic perversity' (Freud's phrase) of childhood eroticism, which knows neither subject nor object. Oedipus is thus a paradoxical choice – a double bind, in other words – between two equally undesirable outcomes: one must accept one's fate and find the means of coming to terms with the lingering anxieties this choice entails, and in this way *resolve* one's Oedipal complex, or else give in to ('fictitious') Oedipal desires and thereby fall into the black hole of neurosis and social ostracism. 'And everybody knows what psychoanalysis means by *resolving* Oedipus: internalising it so as to better rediscover it on the outside, in social authority, where it will be made to proliferate and be passed on to the children.' (AO, 87/94). You get out of your Oedipal 'crisis' by going into it more fully, by accepting its terms and becoming Oedipalized. In this sense, as Deleuze and Guattari point out, Oedipus is both a problem and a solution, and in its thrall one is condemned to a perpetual oscillation between what are effectively the two poles of a single Oedipalizing tendency: either you identify with Oedipus and suffer it as a crisis, or you receive it as a structure and you internalize it as an inner conflict. In other words, there is no question of resolving one's Oedipal crisis, if by that one means setting it aside forever, putting it beyond all thought. It stays with you, burrowing further and further below the surface, blockading the productive unconscious, pulling it up short at every turn.

So, why can't we get out of the Oedipal trap? This brings us to the third paralogism of application. As we saw with the previous paralogism, psychoanalysis rigs the game from the start: it fixes the social field as a point of departure and the family as the point of destination. It assumes that the subject's place in the world, along with their view of the world, and their way of relating to it, is decided, determined and shaped in the family setting. Psychoanalysis treats the subject as though they were perpetually 'sick from their childhood'. But even more tellingly, psychoanalysis assumes that in our childhood it is only the family that matters to us, that in effect we only have eyes for mummy and daddy, as though all our games, dreams and fantasies revolve around nothing but the shuttered-in trinity of mummy-daddy-me. But as they point out, children are surely not unaware of the fact that daddy 'has a boss who is not father's father, or moreover that [their] father himself is a boss who is not a father' (AO, 106/115).

Psychoanalysis assumes that in our unconscious all social relations are viewed through the lens of our childhood, such that even as adults we continue to think of our boss and all other authority figures as being like our father and suffer accordingly. We are thus 'sick from our childhood' in a double sense: not only does our childhood, and its various unresolved neuroses, serve as a constant point of reference for everything that we do as adults, we are constantly falling into new childhoods like so many pits of hell in which we create fresh examples of the same old worries. And thus we come to the fourth paralogism of fictitious desire. 'The law tells us: You will not marry your mother, and you will not kill your father. And we docile subjects say to ourselves: so *that's* what I wanted.' (AO, 125/136). In assuming that if something is prohibited that must mean we secretly desire it, psycho-analysis misunderstands both how desire functions and how law functions. And we shouldn't think this only applies to incest – we must extend this thinking to all prohibitions. It is an error in logic, Deleuze and Guattari argue, to assume it is possible to deduce the nature of what is prohibited from the prohibition itself. For a start, it means assuming that what is prohibited is in fact a real desire, something that we actually long to do, and would not hesitate to do were we not restrained by law. By the same token, it assumes that the prohibition is put in place solely to prevent or at least inhibit from being performed those acts society deems 'improper'. But the reality is, desire is not *that* 'guilty' and the law *that* 'innocent'.

> For what really takes place is that the law prohibits something that is perfectly fictitious in the order of desire or of the 'instincts', so as to persuade its subjects that they had the intention corresponding to the fiction. This is indeed the only way the law has of getting a grip on intention, of making the unconscious guilty. (AO, 125/136)

Oedipus – that is, the incestuous desire for the mother and the associated desire to murder the father – is the bait repression employs to snare *real* desire.

> If desire is repressed, this is not because it is desire for the mother and for the death of the father; on the contrary, desire becomes that only because it is repressed, it takes on that mask only under the reign of the repression that models the mask for it and plasters it on its face. (AO, 126/138)

Deleuze and Guattari dismiss as doubtful the realist objection that one might make at this point that incest is an obstacle to the establishment of society. The real problem, they say, is elsewhere, and that is in the nature of desire itself, which they maintain is revolutionary in its essence: 'no society can tolerate a position of real desire without its structures of exploitation, servitude, and hierarchy being compromised.' (AO, 126-7/138).

So how does the Oedipus trap work? Deleuze and Guattari describe it as a fiendish apparatus with double pincers that leaves the subject no room for manoeuvre whatsoever.

By placing the distorting mirror of incest before desire (that's what you wanted, isn't it?), desire is shamed, stupefied, it is placed in a situation without exit, it is easily persuaded to deny 'itself' in the name of the more important interests of civilisation (what if everyone did the same, what if everyone married his mother or kept his sister for himself? There would no longer be any differentiations, any exchange possible). (AO, 130/142)

There are two forms of repression at work here, which Deleuze and Guattari term 'psychic repression' and 'social repression'. The former is an unconscious operation, it is repression the mind or psychical apparatus applies internally but unknowingly to its instincts; while the latter is a conscious operation, it is repression the mind or psychical apparatus knowingly applies to the desires it thinks it has. Psychoanalysis gives primacy to the former, treating the latter as mere epiphenomena, as though the so-called 'incest taboo' was somehow a natural or spontaneously occurring act of self-censorship. Freud puts Oedipus before culture, before history; every child, regardless of sex, irrespective of where or when they are born, despite all differences of culture, religion, ethnicity, race, class, education and parenting, must resolve their desire to replace mummy or daddy (depending on sex) in their relation with the parent of the opposite sex. Achieving this is the principal aim or function of psychic repression as psychoanalysis conceives it. Social repression, on the Freudian view of things, comes to bear later, in a secondary fashion, to keep in check the manifold 'returns of the repressed' psychic repression is liable to.

Deleuze and Guattari do not accept that psychic repression must, as a matter of course, take this Oedipal form; in effect, they reject the idea that as far as desire and repression goes there is a natural order of things. Psychic repression is an instrument of social repression, they argue. Both bear on the same thing: desiring-production. The question might arise at this point – if psychic repression is an instrument of social repression then why speak of two repressions, why not say there is one form of repression and be done with it? Very simply put, the role of psychic repression is to teach us to desire social repression. In our society, it is the family that 'is the delegated agent of psychic repression, or rather the agent delegated to psychic repression', and 'the incestuous drives are the disfigured image of the repressed' (AO, 130/142). The family is the agent of

Oedipalization, but not the cause. It creates the necessary conditions for Oedipalization and ensures their perpetuation. The family is a stimulus, but it is 'qualitatively indifferent, an inductor that is neither an organiser nor a disorganiser' (AO, 108/117). Although the family has a definite part to play in the Oedipalization of the subject, in the perpetuation of Oedipus in general, Deleuze and Guattari conspicuously do not *blame* the family for either the role it has been given to play in the service of social repression or the way it performs that role. In short, the family isn't a powerful enough machine to bind all its units to itself in such a way that nothing escapes or seeps in to form unauthorized connections. Oedipalization, triangulation, castration, require 'forces a bit more powerful, a bit more subterranean than psychoanalysis, than the family, than ideology, even joined together' (AO, 132/145).

This brings us to the fifth and final paralogism: the failure to recognize that it is desiring-production rather than the Oedipal complex which is the actual or active factor.

The micropolitics of desire

It is at the level of passive synthesis that Deleuze and Guattari's 'micropolitics of desire', as they sometimes call it, actually takes effect, because 'passive synthesis' is synonymous with the Real itself. As far as Deleuze and Guattari are concerned, politics can only go forwards (in the sense of advancing a radical change agenda, even an open-ended one such as the one Deleuze and Guattari propose) by focusing on the mechanisms of desiring-production itself, namely the passive syntheses in all their permutations and arrangements. They reject as imprecise political praxis built on the notion of ideology and in its place offer the three syntheses of connection, disjunction and conjunction as a more efficient means of mapping social and political attitudes.

Desiring-production has two modalities: either an *illegitimate* conformist (i.e., neurotic or sedentary) mode comprised of global and specific syntheses of connection, exclusive or restrictive syntheses of disjunction and segregative and biunivocal syntheses of consumption, or a *legitimate* nonconformist (i.e., schizo or nomadic) mode comprised of partial and non-specific syntheses of connection, inclusive or non-restrictive syntheses of disjunction, and nomadic or polyvocal syntheses of consumption. Determining which of these two modalities is dominant in any particular regime of desiring-production encountered in history is the core of Deleuze and Guattari's political analysis. There are of course stages in between these two poles comprised of mixed permutations of legitimate and illegitimate syntheses such as one finds in most forms of identity politics, which tend to argue for a liberation from the 'global or specific' conception of the self so as to allow for the proliferation of nomadic 'differences' only to police those differences in an 'exclusive or restrictive' manner. Sorting through the inner complexity of different regimes is in effect Deleuze and Guattari's method and mode of what in a more traditional Marxist discourse is known as *Ideologiekritik*. The ultimate practical aim of all such analyses is to figure out how the illegitimate uses of the passive syntheses may be turned around and converted into legitimate uses[32] (AO, 76/80).

What do Deleuze and Guattari mean by legitimate and illegitimate?

> In what he termed the critical revolution, Kant intended to discover criteria immanent to understanding so as to distinguish the legitimate and illegitimate uses of syntheses of consciousness. In the name of transcendental philosophy (immanence of criteria), he therefore denounced the transcendent use of syntheses such as appeared in metaphysics. (AO, 83/89)

Their critique of psychoanalysis, which they define as materialist, proceeds along the same path, 'denouncing the illegitimate use of the syntheses of the unconscious as found in Oedipal psychoanalysis, so as to rediscover a transcendental unconscious defined by the immanence of its criteria' (AO, 83/89). We have already seen what this transcendental unconscious defined by the immanence of its criteria looks like: desiring-production. For Deleuze and Guattari the path to a metaphysics of the unconscious, that is to say a conception of the unconscious defined by transcendent criteria rather than immanent criteria (i.e., criteria imposed upon it rather than discovered within it), is the apparently innocuous sounding question: 'what does it mean?' In order to understand how the unconscious works we have to first of all stop thinking of its productions in terms of meaning. As we saw with Lenz, his delirium contains no meaning as such, only effects – the feeling that he is but one cog in a much larger machine has no meaning, it just is, and for so long as we insist on trying to connect this feeling to something outside and beyond it we will misunderstand the unconscious and fall into metaphysics.

The whole of what might be termed the schizoanalytic 'cure' starts by tracing a line back to the productive unconscious, to the syntheses of desire, because it is only there that it is possible to bring about the necessary reversal of illegitimate syntheses, and the restoration of legitimate syntheses (AO, 123/134). As such, the illegitimate use of the syntheses of desire can be used to triangulate our way back to legitimate uses. The essential principle of this process is that in the history of the unconscious in Lacan's sense (i.e., the history the analysand recounts to the analyst), Oedipus always comes later, like some foreign invader intent upon subduing and civilizing the aboriginal population of the mind. Oedipus is not there from the start, whether as latent structure or future crisis, but rather lays siege to the unconscious from the outside and eventually captures and appropriates to its own purposes all its mechanisms, twisting the syntheses in illegitimate directions. The fact that the three syntheses operate separately, but all at once, means that the capture of just one of the three can be enough to distort the operation of all three. The take-over doesn't need to happen all at once, in a single blow – it can be progressive, degenerative, slow, insidious, and even pleasant. Oedipalization isn't necessarily experienced as repressive – indeed, it can even afford us with the gratification of finally understanding ourselves: 'so that's why I did that!' Through the steady corruption of legitimate uses of the passive syntheses into their opposite, the Western subject was produced as the paranoid egomaniac we know him to be. For this reason, as I will try to show in greater detail in what follows, the illegitimate syntheses should in fact be the principal focus, at least in the first instance, of any schizoanalysis concerned with an understanding of contemporary culture.

The illegitimate syntheses

The illegitimate synthesis of connection
The first illegitimate use of the syntheses, which Deleuze and Guattari also designate as the first of psychoanalysis's five paralogisms, relates to the Lacanian concept of lack.

We are told that partial objects are caught up in an intuition of precocious totality, just as the ego is caught up in an intuition of unity that precedes its fulfilment. (Even in Melanie Klein, the schizoid partial object is related to a whole that prepares for the advent of the complete object in the depressive phase.) It is clear that such a totality-unity is posited only in terms of a certain mode of absence, as that which partial objects and subjects of desire 'lack'. (AO, 81/86)

Why does this constitute an illegitimate use of the *synthesis of connection*? Let us take a concrete example – the killer shark in *Jaws* (Spielberg, 1975). As both Fredric Jameson and (after him) Slavoj Žižek have argued, we fundamentally misunderstand the function of the shark if we start by assuming it is an allegory of something in particular.[33] While it is obviously true that the shark could stand for US imperialism (Fidel Castro's suggestion) or communism itself (to vouch for the other side of that ideological divide), with the besieged island of Amity standing for America itself in all its clichéd glory – exuberant teenagers, curmudgeonly small business owners, corrupt politicians, a conflicted cop who loves his wife, and so on – the very multiplicity of possibilities suggests that the true vocation of the shark 'lies less in any single message or meaning than in its very capacity to absorb and organise all these quite distinct anxieties together'.[34] Following Jameson's lead, Žižek argues that the shark is phallic for precisely the reason that it has no meaning in itself, but gives rise to the illusion that the text as a whole has meaning because of its presence. As Žižek puts it, the shark is a perfect example of 'what Lacan calls a *"point de capiton"*: the emergence of the shark as symbol does not add any new meaning, it simply reorganises meanings which were already there by binding them to the same signifier'.[35] What resists this binding is our fascination for and our *enjoyment* of the shark's terrifying presence – Žižek then draws the perfectly Deleuzian conclusion that you cannot have both meaning and enjoyment in the one symbol, the former cancels out the latter (AO, 177/190).

The presence of the shark changes the way all the elements in the set called Amity Island relate to each other. It brings out all the class and generational antagonisms that propel the drama towards its end, which isn't the defeat of the shark but the acceptance of something they all have in common and equally lack, call it 'community spirit' or 'civic feeling' or whatever. In the midst of the crisis people relate to one another according to their interests and what amounts to the same thing, their position in society, which in Deleuze and Guattari's terms renders them 'global' and 'specific'. This point will become clearer if we perform a Žižekian experiment and imagine *Jaws* without the shark.[36] Minus the shark, there would still be the same inter-generational conflicts between 'spring break' college students partying on the beach and the prudish long-term residents of Amity, the cop would still be the same burnt-out case looking for a reason to believe in humanity, and the politicians would be just as corrupt. Without the shark, these disparate, molecular desires (the desire to party, the desire for propriety, and so on) would continue to operate side by side, if not in harmony then not necessarily in conflict either, their endogenous status unchallenged, each of them operating without much regard for the others and according to their own internal dynamic. Obviously the appearance of the shark changes everything – relations that had hitherto been endogenous are suddenly brought into the sphere of an exogenous force, namely the shark, and the disparate desires are made to seem 'selfish', which is to say 'lacking' in 'community spirit'. The shark is both castrating *and* phallic – it first of all denies the island of Amity its usual points of cathexis: it prohibits the pleasures of swimming, sailing, skiing and so forth, and that in turn inhibits the capitalist's pleasure in drawing off a surplus profit from these pleasures, and that creates conflict which upsets the placid life of the cop who just wants to keep the peace. But even more importantly, whereas these disparate pleasures used to seem independent parts of no part, they now appear to be the disconnected parts of an absent whole. It is the acceptance of this perspective that is phallic because it reorganizes the very function and distribution of desire.[37]

That the scenario which confronts us in the hypothetical shark-free Amity seems ripe for the kind of transformation the dramatic entrance of the shark realizes, and simply boring without it, can perhaps be taken as a measure of the degree to which we are already Oedipalized. For what we expect as viewers is precisely the proper Oedipalization of all this untamed desiring-production. The arc of the narrative does not go from idyll through trauma back to idyll, nor indeed from unresolved conflict and anxiety through cathartic trauma to idyll (psychoanalysis makes both of these options available to us, as does traditional narratology); but on the contrary, it goes from a patently schizo situation of molecular desire through trauma to arrive at a proper renunciation of desire and a weary resignation before the law. The longed-for ideological pay-off of the film, i.e., the generic moment when the town sets aside all its petty-seeming differences and agrees to work together, apparently united in a common cause (though in fact their cause remains purely individual because their motivation is survival[38]), is a perfect illustration of Deleuze and Guattari's thesis that it is castration that gives rise to the phallus. A shark-free Amity is easy to imagine because the scenario of a small town rife with petty rivalries and seemingly in need of something or someone to pull it together is so familiar, as indeed is the inevitable conclusion. *Jaws* is basically a western – it has all the requisite generic elements: isolated small town dependent on the nature for its prosperity (in this case the sea as a tourist attraction), competing interests amongst the townsfolk, a disaffected but expert sheriff, and a threatening outsider. The story unfolds and climaxes exactly as you would expect of a western. My point is that the shark, fully as much as the demonized Native Americans in actual westerns, is not meaningful in itself; it is a mechanism whose purpose is to bring about a connective synthesis. It is, however, an illegitimate synthesis because it determines in advance what its final form should be and passes judgement on all who come before it in the name of that final form. Insofar as the narrative constantly points to the lack of 'community spirit', the failure to act collectively for the common good, as the true cause of the disaster that unfolds, it imposes that sense of 'precocious totality' mentioned above which has the invidious effect of making individuals caught up in its current feel incomplete.[39]

Looked at from the point of view of function rather than meaning, the principal desire in this narrative trope is the desire for membership in the 'fused group' (to use Sartre's notion). It is this 'fused group' or 'precocious totality', which lies at the heart of the drama, not the shark. This is not to say the shark is unimportant. But its importance lies less in what it might stand for than its purpose and more especially the fact that its purpose is itself subject to a festishistic appropriation. As Deleuze and Guattari maintain with regards to Oedipus, it would not have the hold on Western society it does if it were not desired; the same must be said for the shark: the fear it provokes in us is desired. The lack of 'community spirit' is paradoxical in this regard because it is also clear that the reason the 'community spirit' is lacking is that until now there had been no reason for it to exist. In this sense, what is truly felt as lacking is in fact the shark itself, the 'common enemy', because only by power of its menace can the island come together without having to renounce individual interest. This longing is of course realized in the subsequent sequels and copycat films that were made in the wake of *Jaws'* phenomenal box-office success. But it is also to be found in virtually every disaster movie ever made in Hollywood. That it is a peculiarly American trope can perhaps be seen in the utterly emblematic moment in *Independence Day* (Emmerich, 1996) when Bill Pullman, playing an ex-fighter pilot turned President of the United States, rallies the troops with a rousing speech in which it is clear that fighting back against the alien intruders is the American way and that America equals the world. One can really only understand westerns properly when it is grasped that the indigenous other is always regarded as an intruder, an invader from afar, who has no right to the land that manifest destiny put in the hands of white Americans. The same is obviously true of the shark in *Jaws*, it too is treated as an alien invader with no right to be where it is.

The illegitimate synthesis of disjunction
The peculiar effects of the illegitimate uses of the disjunctive synthesis are everywhere to be seen throughout literature and culture for the simple reason that as we saw in the previous chapter this is the supreme form of ideology itself. Hence the question which animates so much of *Anti-Oedipus*: 'Given a certain effect, what machine is capable of producing it?' This question has the somewhat surprising vocation of leading us towards what Jameson calls a 'dialectical reversal', the paradoxical effect whereby what looked like a solution or an achieved fact turns out to be nothing other than a question in disguise. It is surprising because given Deleuze's famous declarations concerning his hatred of dialectics, it might be thought that such effects would be anathema to Deleuze. But in fact the whole of *Anti-Oedipus* can be construed as one long dialectical reversal inasmuch as it seizes on the Oedipal complex, which for psychoanalysis is the solution to the problem of how desire functions, and transforms it into a problem all over again by asking how and under what conditions we came to think of ourselves as Oedipalized. Any lingering doubt on this score is dispelled by the endorsement given to Marx's *On the Jewish Question*, one of the great examples of dialectic analysis (AO, 89/96). The synthesis of disjunction is the mechanism that produces both the effect we refer to as 'the subject' and the hailing effect known as 'interpellation' which positions that subject

in the social. As is the case with all the passive syntheses, the synthesis of disjunction is subject to both a legitimate (inclusive) and illegitimate (exclusive) use, the latter being the more common.

The Oedipalized subject – that is, the subject whose sexuality is defined by the parental triangle of daddy-mommy-me – offers the perfect example of the effect of the illegitimate or exclusive use of the synthesis of disjunction. Oedipus works in two directions at once, which is to say it entails two different types of disjunctive synthesis. To begin with, 'Oedipus informs us: if you don't follow the lines of differentiation daddy-mommy-me, and the exclusive alternatives that delineate them, you will fall into the black night of the undifferentiated.' (AO, 87/93). Having imposed this first dualism, and forced us to choose the differentiated realm of the symbolic over the undifferentiated realm of the imaginary (i.e., the adult realm of language and expression over the infantile realm of imagination and fantasy), Oedipus forces us to internalize a second dualism, namely the distinction between self and other, along with the assumption that the other is irreducibly different from the self. Oedipus 'forces desire to take as its object the differentiated parental persons, and, brandishing the threats of the undifferentiated, prohibits the correlative ego from satisfying its desires with these persons, in the name of the same requirements of differentiation' (AO, 87/93). This is, then, the second of the five paralogisms Deleuze and Guattari identify in psychoanalysis: as both a problem and a solution, Oedipus is an instance of what Gregory Bateson referred to as a 'double bind' (AO, 88/94). The essential form of the exclusive use of the synthesis of disjunction is 'either/or' – either I am a man or a woman, young or old, alive or dead, and so on.

> Everywhere in psychoanalysis, in Freud, we have seen this taste for exclusive disjunctions assert itself. It becomes nevertheless apparent that schizophrenia teaches us a singular extra-Oedipal lesson, and reveals to us an unknown force of the disjunctive synthesis, an immanent use that would no longer be exclusive or restrictive, but fully affirmative, non-restrictive, inclusive. (AO, 84/90)

This, Deleuze and Guattari admit, is perhaps the greatest logical paradox we can conceive: a disjunction that separates terms without at the same time using one to negate the other. Its form is 'either . . . or . . . or' and as Deleuze and Guattari illustrate examples of it are to be found in the work of Beckett, Nijinsky, Rimbaud, as well as many others.

I am God I am not God, I am God I am Man: it is not a matter of a synthesis that would go beyond the negative disjunctions of the derived reality, in an original reality of Man-God, but rather of an inclusive disjunction that carries out the synthesis itself in drifting from one term to another and following the distance between terms. (AO, 86/92)

How is this possible? Everything depends on how one conceives of the terms themselves. To the schizophrenic, according to Deleuze and Guattari, the names of history do not designate persons living or dead, but states of intensity, or 'effects' – God is the *feeling* of omnipotence, divine fury, judgement, and so on, while Napoleon might be the *feeling* of triumph, persecution, victory, defeat and so on.

This can be clearly seen in physics, where proper names designate such effects within fields of potentials: the Joule effect, the Seebeck effect, the Kelvin effect. History is like physics: a Joan of Arc effect, a Heliogabalus effect – all the *names* of history, and not the name of the father. (AO, 95/103)

By invoking these names the schizophrenic is able to *feel* their power and collects a 'fraudulent premium' from his avatars (AO, 97/105). He does not identify with any of these figures, nor think of himself as being any of the people he names; they are just so many singularities to be passed through as rapidly as possible.

The schizophrenic is dead *or* alive, not both at once, but each of the two as the terminal point of a distance over which he glides. He is child *or* parent, not both, but the one at the end of the other, like the two ends of a stick in a nondecomposable space. This is the meaning of the disjunctions where Beckett records his characters and the events that befall them: *everything divides, but into itself.* (AO, 85/90–1)

TV melodramas are precisely schizophrenic in this sense – the great TV couples are those which constantly traverse the nondecomposable space of the question 'will they or won't they', which is the dramatic cognate of 'either . . . or . . . or'. This nondecomposable space is of course the body without organs (or what we have termed following Althusser the 'plane of obviousness') on which all the operations of the synthesis of disjunction always take place. And as every TV producer knows, creating and preserving this nondecomposable space is essential to the success of the show. Romantic couples become boring the minute they step outside of this space and become simply neurotic. One of the greatest examples of this is the 1980s TV series that gave Bruce Willis his big start, *Moonlighting*. The tension between his character and Cybil Shepherd's was wonderfully intense until they became a couple in the official sense and after that the show lost all its energy. The minute they stopped loving/hating one another and agreed to work out their problems in a rational manner the show lost its point. Their interminable bickering and priapic flirting *was* the point, its nondecomposable space, it was what made the show interesting. When they started making up after fights and carrying through on their suggestive comments, the nature of their disjunctive relationship underwent a profound change: it went from being inclusive and nonrestrictive to exclusive and restrictive. Suddenly their feelings had to be clearly defined (love or hate), their actions clearly specified (sex or not-sex), and in the process all intensity was flushed away. So the perfect combination, from this perspective, as realized in the case of Mulder and Scully in *The X-Files*, say, or Dawson and Joey in *Dawson's Creek*, Buffy and Angel in *Buffy the Vampire Slayer*, Clark and Lana in *Smallville*, even Xena and Gabriele in *Xena: The Warrior Princess*, is for the characters to act according to their desire but *never* acknowledge it. Paradoxically, by not acknowledging their desire, by refusing to yield to society's demand that desire must be boxed up in categories, the subjects remain free to inhabit the non-decomposable space of intensity we call 'love'.

The implicit practical problem in the foregoing example is this: how do we move from the synthesis of disjunction to the body without organs? The complication is that the real power of the body without organs is its ability to make it appear that the problems it poses (i.e., the syntheses of disjunction) can only be solved according to the conditions it specifies. Thus capitalist ideologues have been able to represent the problem of Third World poverty as a problem of distribution – the problem of insufficient capital in a particular place, the sprawling slums of Lagos, say, whose inhabitants survive on less than a dollar a day, or less than what most Westerners cheerfully spend on a cup of coffee – rather than a problem of causation – the problem of too much capitalism, and the absence of an alternative political model, rather than not enough capital. Capital is in this sense both the problem and the solution, which is why Deleuze and Guattari insist that the only way out of this deadlock is to reject both the problem *and* the solution.[40] The most efficient way of doing this, as Jameson shows in his reading of Joseph Conrad's *Lord Jim* (to borrow yet another concrete example from him), particularly his analysis of the theme of *ressentiment*, is to treat the solution as a problem in its own right. The choice of example is not accidental or simply expedient. As Jameson demonstrates in *The Political Unconscious*, Deleuze and Guattari's famous injunction against asking what a text means can be read as an injunction against 'ethical criticism' (Jameson's term), that is literary and cultural criticism concerned to interrogate either the meaning of human existence (e.g., 'metaphysics') or human nature (e.g., 'humanism').[41] Although both of these schools of thought – metaphysics and humanism – have been roundly criticized, almost into extinction, by Derrida and Althusser respectively, that doesn't mean they have lost their relevance in everyday life, where they survive in the hardiest form of all as untested 'opinions'.[42] 'In its narrowest sense, ethical thought projects as permanent features of human "experience", and thus a kind of "wisdom" about personal life and interpersonal relations, what are in reality the historical and institutional specifics of a determinate type of group solidarity or class cohesion.'[43] In other words, such approaches to understanding culture obscure the real work of desiring-production behind a smokescreen of 'effects'.

Jameson's starting point, as we might expect, is to refuse to accept the obviousness of the motivation of Conrad's tale, which supposedly centres on Jim's loss of honour following the *Patna* episode (in which Jim disgraces himself as a man of the sea by jumping overboard to escape a ship that wasn't actually sinking) and his convoluted bid both to outrun his shame and at the same time regain his self-esteem, firstly by being the most audacious chandler afloat and then later on (and decisively) by showing selfless courage in the attack on Patusan. Typically for Conrad, whose work is sometimes described as expressionistic, the story is quite self-consciously the dramatization of a concept (e.g., honour) – to use Deleuze's notion from his book on Nietzsche – but, Jameson argues, if we go along with this, then we are accepting Conrad's strategy of ideological containment and allowing ourselves to be seduced by the plane of obviousness he tempts us with. To counter this temptation, Jameson suggests we ask ourselves, 'why we should be expected to assume, in the midst of capitalism, that the aesthetic rehearsal of the problematics of a social value from a quite different mode of production – the feudal ideology of honour – should need no justification and should be expected to be of interest to us'.[44] To put this in Deleuze and Guattari's terms, what Jameson is effectively saying is that we will misunderstand what is really going on in *Lord Jim* if we fail to consider the nature of the relation between the surface level synthesis of disjunction, namely the matter of Jim's honour, and the more deeply set level of the body without organs, which is the question of why Jim's honour should matter to us in the first place and indeed how and why other perhaps less arcane issues do not occupy our attention instead. Determining the nature of the relation between a particular synthesis of disjunction and the body without organs on which it operates is what I am calling the Deleuzian equivalent of a 'dialectical reversal'. This demands, as Jameson explains, that we grasp the conceptual antinomy of the disjunctive synthesis from below, as it were, i.e., from the level of its historical context, as a contradiction.[45]

In order for me to explain this unfamiliar presentation of Deleuze's thought, I need to add in here the reminder that Deleuze and Guattari (twice) present the body without organs as the master syllogism, by which they mean it appears as the third or transcendent term that unites and resolves a pair of opposites such as one finds in an ethical binary (AO, 14/19; 84/90). This will perhaps be clearer if we refer to another concrete example, the distinction between good and evil let's say. As Nietzsche has shown, this distinction doesn't come from nowhere; it presupposes not only the idea that it is possible to assign values to actions and behaviours, but the desire as well as the power to do so (NP, 119–22/136–40). The determination of good and evil is not self-evident, but invariably follows the interests of the powerful, as is apparent in the US today where Christian fundamentalism is lauded as the good and every other religious fundamentalism, but especially Muslim fundamentalism, is decried out of hand as evil. The powerful use the good and evil syllogism to hide their interest. By acting as though the basis of the distinction is obvious (in the Althusserian sense we have already enunciated), power can validate its actions, however egregious, simply by claiming it is trying to abide by a universally recognized objective distinction.

Witness the US's justification of its invasion of Iraq in 2003 on the grounds that it was acting pre-emptively to preserve democracy and freedom. Thus, as Jameson puts it, 'we have forgotten the thrust of Nietzsche's thought and lost everything scandalous and virulent about it if we cannot understand how it is ethics itself which is the ideological vehicle and the legitimation of concrete structures of power and domination'.[46] Jameson extends the thrust of this observation to Nietzsche himself, arguing that Nietzsche's solution to the problem, his famous 'transvaluation of all values' supposed to take us 'beyond good and evil' (undoubtedly his most famous slogan) leaves intact the problem of why such an ethical binary was required in the first place.

The problem here, for Jameson, is Nietzsche's theory of *ressentiment*, which is supposed to explain how the good and evil binary was constructed. The Christian ideas of charity, resignation and abnegation are, according to Nietzsche, the product of a slave mentality and their purpose is to castrate the strong by making reaction (e.g., giving to the needy) the only authentic form of action. '*Ressentiment* is the triumph of the weak *as* weak, the revolt of the slaves and their victory *as* slaves.' (NP, 117/134). Nietzsche conceives *ressentiment* as the spirit or force that prevents the strong – or, at any rate, those who would be strong – from acting rather than reacting.

> Nietzsche's whole vision of history, his historical master narrative, is organised around this proposition, which diagnoses ethics in general and the Judeo-Christian tradition in particular as a revenge of the slaves upon the masters and an ideological ruse whereby the former infect the latter with a slave mentality – the ethos of charity – in order to rob them of their natural vitality and aggressive, properly aristocratic insolence.[47]

It is at this point, though, that Jameson and Deleuze diverge in their apprehension of Nietzsche. For Jameson, the secondary adaptations of Nietzsche's thought – in Taine, for instance – reveal its deeper political purpose, which not to put too fine a word on it is nothing less than 'counter-revolutionary'. Think of the way trade unions are denigrated by the Right for their selfish behaviour in exercising their collective bargaining power so as to extract better working conditions even as it celebrates the allegedly virtuous selfishness of individual employment contracts as a victory for freedom. In both cases the theory of *ressentiment* as the triumph of the weak *as* weak is mobilized by the strong against the weak in the name of a putatively objective value behind which interest hides its face. *Ressentiment*, then, is a means of coding the 'flow' of the revolutionary impulse so that it appears self-discrediting.[48]

How does this help us to understand *Lord Jim*? The problem of honour inevitably evokes the theme of *ressentiment*, not least because of its pre-eminence in intellectual circles at the time the novel was written. In order to retrieve his lost honour, Jim has to first of all conquer the sea, which he duly does (as I mentioned before) by becoming an audacious chandler, invariably getting out to the ships in harbour first, regardless of weather. But this isn't sufficient, he also needs a human adversary for his transformation to be complete, which is where the ominous *homme de ressentiment* Gentleman Brown fits into the picture. His is that pure form of evil against which even the feeblest attempt to strike a blow can be construed as positive. Instructively enough, Conrad calls Brown 'a blind accomplice of the Dark Powers', thereby exposing his narratological role as well as his inner character.[49] He is needed to compel Jim to act, to finally put the welfare of others before his own and redeem himself. In other words, both Jim and Gentleman Brown mark out regions on the body without organs called 'honour' which through the world-weary mouthpiece of Marlow the text constantly calls on us to treat in an exclusive and restrictive way, as though they were not indeed both products of the same impulse, namely the desire to submerge knowledge of the structural transformation of daily life by the agencies of capitalism beneath a reassuringly chivalric story about the deeds of individuals. And it is imputed, too, that we as readers are too full of *ressentiment* ourselves to appreciate the real majesty of Jim's achievements.[50] The schizophrenic reading, then, the one that brings about the dialectical reversal I mentioned, is the one that treats the gap between Jim and Brown as a nondecomposable space and their relationship as inclusive and non-restrictive.

The illegitimate synthesis of conjunction

If *Lord Jim* isn't an example of a schizophrenic text in Deleuze and Guattari's sense of the word, but is merely susceptible to a schizophrenic reading such as the one I have briefly sketched above, it is because at its core it is dominated by the illegitimate segregative and biunivocal use of the synthesis of conjunction. The entire tale is predicated by Marlow's judgement, pronounced about a third way through the novel – though in point of fact, narrating the moment when he first clapped eyes on Jim. 'He was the right sort; he was one of us.'[51] (This, I take it, is simply the third person permutation of 'So it's *me*!' which is the essential form of the synthesis of conjunction.) The same judgement motivated the earlier *Heart of Darkness*, which served as our introduction to Marlow and was intended by Conrad to function as a foil for *Lord Jim*. Kurtz is, in effect, a Lord Jim, too, the difference being that he is also a Gentleman Brown. It is the absence of a nondecomposable space between Kurtz and his Other that makes *Heart of Darkness* such a different kind of tale on an affective level, although as I want to stress here its structure is the same. Kurtz, too, was 'one of us'. Conrad's insight, which is perfectly consistent with Deleuze and Guattari's analyses, is that the latter yields the former.

> Oedipus [i.e., the 'one' with whom we make our 'us'] depends on this sort of nationalistic, religious, racist sentiment, and not the reverse: it is not the father who is projected onto the boss, but the boss who is applied to the father, either in order to tell us 'you will not surpass your father', or 'you will repress him to find our forefathers'. (AO, 114/123)

Segregation of this nationalistic, religious, racist, type is not a consequence of Oedipus, Deleuze and Guattari argue, but its precondition. The social field could not be 'reduced to the familial tie except by presupposing an enormous archaism, an incarnation of the race in person or in spirit: yes, I am one of you.' (AO, 114/123). This, as we shall see, is ultimately a matter of what Deleuze and Guattari call 'group fantasy' – the legitimate and illegitimate syntheses of conjunction correspond to its counter-revolutionary and revolutionary poles.

When the notion of group fantasy was elaborated in the perspective of institutional analysis – in the works of the team at La Borde Clinic, assembled around Jean Oury – the first task was to show it differed from individual fantasy. It became evident that group fantasy was inseparable from the 'symbolic' articulations that define a social field insofar as it is real, whereas the individual fantasy fitted the whole of this field over 'imaginary' givens. If this first distinction is drawn out, we see that the individual fantasy is itself plugged into the existing social field, but apprehends it in the form of imaginary qualities that confer on it a kind of transcendence or immortality under the shelter of which the individual, the ego, plays out its pseudo destiny: what does it matter if I die, says the general, since the Army is immortal? (AO, 70/73)

It is important to Jim that his honour be restored because without that he wouldn't have the consolation of its immortality. The immortality of the institutions we venerate is, according to Deleuze and Guattari, the psychic vector that installs in the ego

all the investments of repression, the phenomena of identification, of 'superegoization' and castration, all the resignation-desires (becoming a general; acquiring low, middle, or high rank), including the resignation to dying in the service of this order, whereas the drive itself is projected onto the outside and turned against the others (death to the foreigner, to those who are not of our own ranks!). (AO, 70/74)

Our identification with the institutions of power in the familial fashion Deleuze and Guattari describe here is not attributable to the fact that Oedipus is a universal and therefore we are unable to relate to power except in this way. Deleuze and Guattari's point is that if we happen to think of the Army as daddy it is because power has learned that this is a highly efficient way of obtaining our docility. This is the reason Oedipus is apparently everywhere, it serves a useful purpose. (The key historical question asked by *Anti-Oedipus*, which I will deal with more fully in the next section, is: how did we become susceptible to Oedipus?)

The revolutionary pole of group fantasy becomes visible, on the contrary, in the power to experience institutions themselves as mortal, to destroy them or change them according to the articulations of desire and the social field, by making the death instinct into a veritable institutional creativity. For that is precisely the criterion – at least the formal criterion – that distinguishes the revolutionary institution from the enormous inertia which the law communicates to institutions in an established order. As Nietzsche says; churches, armies, States – which of all these dogs wants to die? (AO, 70–1/74)

Is this not what all the colonial writers – from Kipling to Conrad to Forster – feared most? That the empire and all its institutions might prove to be not merely mortal, but sadly all too human as well? Is this not the 'white man's burden', the constant need to prop up the fantasy if not the actual reality of the immortal empire? Was this not 'the horror, the horror' of Kurtz's dying breath? And can we not see Forster's emblematic exhortation 'only connect' as the desperate plea of an individual fantasy that desires nothing so much as to be properly plugged into a group fantasy, something able to confer the feeling of immortality and relieve the ego of its anxiety. Group fantasy incorporates into itself the various syntheses of disjunction which cause our lives to be led in an exclusive and restrictive manner, 'in the sense that each subject, discharged of his personal identity but not of his singularities, enters into relations with others following the communication proper to partial objects [synthesis of connection]: everyone passes into the body of the other on the body without organs' (AO, 71/74).

SAVAGES, BARBARIANS, CIVILIZED MEN

Hence the goal of schizoanalysis: to analyse the specific nature of the libidinal investments in the economic and political spheres, and thereby to show how, in the subject who desires, desire can be made to desire its own repression – whence the role of the death drive in the circuit connecting desire to the social sphere.

Gilles Deleuze and Félix Guattari, *Anti-Oedipus*

How then should we go about analysing the specific nature of the libidinal investments in the economic and politic spheres? This means reaching the point where we can grasp the fact 'the economic, the political, and the religious are things that are invested by the libido for themselves' and not as derivatives of 'mommy-daddy' (AO, 200/216). Reaching this point is, Deleuze and Guattari instruct, a two-step operation: first we need to study social institutions, or what they refer to as 'molar aggregates', and find out what they mean; second, one needs to go beyond, or get beneath, these molar aggregates, by searching for the 'molecular elements' constituting the various desiring-machines that compose and motivate them.

> One searches for the way in which these machines *function*, for how they invest and underdetermine (*subdéterminent*) the social machines that they constitute on a large scale. One then reaches the regions of a productive, molecular, micrological, or microphysical unconscious that no longer represents anything. (AO, 200/216)

In this domain of the productive unconscious, sexuality ceases to be a matter of relations between whole or global persons and instead defines a molecular energy powering the three syntheses:

> For desiring-machines are precisely that: the microphysics of the unconscious, the elements of the microunconscious. But as such they never exist independently of the historical molar aggregates, of the macroscopic social formations that they constitute statistically. In this sense there is only desire and the social. Beneath the conscious investments of economic, political, religious, etc., formations, there are unconscious sexual investments, microinvestments that attest to the way in which desire is present in a social field, and joins this field to itself as the statistically determined domain that is bound to it. (AO, 200/216)

Admittedly, as methodological instruction goes, this gives us very little to be going on with, but it does at least offer a clue as to their social ontology, which is a very useful place to start.

This history of social machines has a dual purpose. On the one hand, it is an account of the coming into being of capitalism; on the other hand, it is a genealogy of the contemporary structure of desire. The three regimes – the primitive territorial regime, the despotic regime and the modern capitalist regime – correspond to the three points of Lacan's triadic mapping of the structure, namely the Real, the Symbolic and the Imaginary. Perhaps the most striking aspect of this genealogy is their repositioning of the Symbolic as the domain of latency and the Imaginary as the realization of desire's trajectory. Their conclusion is precisely that in contemporary society desire is trapped in a simulacral universe of mommy-daddy-me (AO, 286/315). When Deleuze and Guattari say that *Anti-Oedipus* was intended to assist Lacan, to give him some help, what they mean is this: they ground his concepts in history, thus answering the question Lacan himself left unanswered, namely the question of the genealogy of his concepts (AO, 290/319). In the process, what they aim to show is that it is capitalism itself that gives rise to Oedipus as the dirty little secret of desire. The aim isn't to exonerate desire and profess its innocence, however, but to show that it is primarily social in nature.

> Yes, Oedipus is nevertheless the universal of desire, the product of universal history – but on one condition, which is not met by Freud: that Oedipus be capable, at least to a certain point, of conducting its autocritique. Universal history is nothing more than a theology if it does not seize control of the conditions of the contingent, singular existence, its irony, and its own critique. And what are these conditions, this point where the autocritique is possible and necessary? To discover beneath the familial reduction the nature of the social investments of the unconscious. To discover beneath the individual fantasy the nature of group fantasies. (AO, 294/323)

This, finally, is what this chapter sets out to do: it shows that the personalization of desire represented by Lacan's triad is an effect of a social machine, not a point of origin.

The ontology of social machines

Social machines are statistically constituted and follow a law of large numbers (AO, 316/342). What do Deleuze and Guattari mean by this? It is a code phrase implying that the social formation is brought into being by the accumulation or aggregation of desiring-machines, but the net result of this process cannot be understood in linear terms. In *A Thousand Plateaus* they explain their approach in Darwinian terms, rejecting the inherent idealism of those histories which grasp social formations in terms of degrees of development or types of forms in favour of populations and coefficients of speed. Forms do not precede or pre-exist populations, they are more like their statistical result.

Thus the relationship between embryogenesis and phylogenesis is reversed: the embryo does not testify to an absolute form preestablished in a closed milieu; rather, the phylogenesis of populations has at its disposal, in an open milieu, an entire range of relative forms to choose from, none of which is preestablished. (ATP, 54/64)

By the same token, the degrees of development are not degrees of perfection measured against a pre-existing template or model, but states of equilibrium in a more or less constant movement of variation whose end result cannot be known. 'Degrees are no longer measured in terms of increasing perfection or a differentiation and increase in the complexity of the parts, but in terms of differential relations and coefficients such as selective pressure, catalytic action, speed of propagation, rate of growth, evolution, mutation, etc.' (ATP, 54/64). Essentially what Deleuze and Guattari are arguing here is this: the movement of microscopic entities combines to produce macroscopic entities which in turn react on those same microscopic entities, forcing them to adapt and change. As a simple example of this, one can look at the notions of the crowd, herd or swarm: all three are composed of x number of individual beings who by themselves act quite differently to how they act in a group. To put it another way, the behaviour of the individual components of these three forms taken on their own is not a reliable indicator of the behaviour of the crowd, herd or swarm. As is well known perfectly docile men and women can behave with extraordinary courage or equally extraordinary violence once swept up in a crowd.

But crowds aren't true social formations inasmuch as they are ephemeral gatherings of people, living and dying with the moment. If anything they are more like limit-points of social formations, moments of rupture with the potential to engulf and drown an existing social system. And throughout Deleuze and Guattari's work, particularly in their accounts of schizo delirium, the crowd, herd or swarm function emblematically as a kind of anti-social form, a form of collectivity whose internal bonds are differently configured to those of bourgeoise society in the era of late capitalism. True social formations are more enduring than crowds and it is precisely the problem of how they endure, or rather how they are made to be more enduring than spontaneous irruptions like crowds, that is central to this chapter of *Anti-Oedipus*. Deleuze and Guattari's thesis in this regard, though complex in its details, is in fact relatively simple and not unfamiliar in its thrust: social formations come into being and endure by capturing and coding the flows of desire. They are in this precise sense machines, but in contrast to technical machines which extend man's capacity to undertake defined tasks social machines incorporate man himself into its mechanisms (AO, 155/165). As such, their formation is not simply a matter of 'scaling up', that is going from a small group of persons to a large group of persons, or even from a single individual to an entire nation. Here it is worth observing that although it purports to be Deleuze and Guattari inspired (but readily admits to its own originality), Manuel DeLanda's 'assemblage theory', is in fact nothing other than a theory of 'scaling up'.[52] What DeLanda excises from Deleuze and Guattari's theory is *the difference in kind* between the two regimes of desiring-production: that is, between desiring-production in its 'free labour' or schizo phase and desiring-production in its 'primitive accumulation' phase. He correctly emphasizes that since the first book on David Hume it has been part of Deleuze's doctrine that relations are external to their terms, but neglects the fact that in what Deleuze refers to as a 'field of immanence' (such as one encounters in the schizo delirium) terms cease to function as they do in a transcendental field. In a 'field of immanence' all relations are interior to their terms inasmuch that the terms themselves are simply states of intensity through which desire passes (TRM, 384–9/359–63). There is no 'scaling up' from the schizo delirium to the social field, instead one has to bring about an alteration in the regime of desiring-production for change to occur. In other words, what DeLanda eliminates from Deleuze and Guattari is desire itself.[53]

The first capture of desiring-production, that is to say the social machine was the territorial machine. Invented by the so-called 'primitive peoples' it has now disappeared in most if not all places in the world, surviving here and there only as a revenant, something thought to be long dead but somehow still with us. Capitalism is built on the ruins of social formations like the territorial machine that went before it, mobilizing their eviscerated structures to its own ends. In this precise sense it is correct, Deleuze and Guattari argue, to 'understand all of history in the light of capitalism, provided that the rules formulated by Marx are followed exactly' (AO, 153/163). Principally, this means recognizing that history is contingent not necessary (its necessity is always after the fact), that it comprises a long sequence of accidents, mishaps, chance meetings and unexpected syntheses, rather than a logical progression from one kind of society to another, or from conditions of scarcity to conditions of plenitude. More especially, it means recognizing that history is discontinuous; it is made up of ruptures and limits, breaks and transformations, not continuity or progress.

> For great accidents were necessary, and amazing encounters that could have happened elsewhere, or before, or might never have happened, in order for the flows to escape coding and, escaping, to nonetheless fashion a new machine bearing the determinations of the capitalist socius. (AO, 154/163)

And as will be seen in more detail in what follows this is exactly the way Deleuze and Guattari narrate the history of the formation of capitalism. Deleuze and Guattari's hypothesis, which structures their entire account of the genealogy of social forms is this: capitalism was known to the primitive peoples as that which would destroy their society and their rituals were designed to preserve them from this menace. 'If capitalism is the universal truth, it is so in the sense that makes capitalism *the negative* of all social formations.' (AO, 168/180). Thus the two regimes preceding capitalism, the territorial machine and the despotic machine, can be understood as 'negations of negations' (to use Hegel's concept) in that their structures are designed to inhibit the irruption of capitalism's free-flowing flows.

This hypothesis has three components. First, it assumes that desire is essentially gregarious in nature, inasmuch that as humans we seem driven to want to live in groups. Deleuze and Guattari arrive at this point in a classically dialectical manner, namely via what Hegel referred to as the path of the negative (*via negativa*). If desire was not gregarious, not part of the very infrastructure of society, then, they reason, we could not explain how it is possible for people to fight for their own oppression. But, by the same token, desire is not bonding, it may bring a group together but it will not necessarily enable the group to endure. Man is in this sense simultaneously *Homo natura* and *Homo historia*. This is the second assumption: desire has to be trained or disciplined to produce lasting collectivities (AO, 208/227). For this reason, all social formations prior to capitalism viewed the flows of desire as dangerous and they dealt with this danger by a practice Deleuze and Guattari refer to as 'coding'. 'Flows of women and children, flows of herds and of seed, sperm flows, flows of shit, menstrual flows: nothing must escape coding.' (AO, 156/166). This is the third assumption: desire is socialized by codification (i.e., the attribution of meaning). Women, children, herds, seed, sperm, shit, menstrual blood and so on are transformed into gifts from God, or given some other symbolic value and thereby given a social function they did not previously have. This is what coding is at its most basic. When Deleuze and Guattari say we should not ask about the meaning of something, they are referring only to the operations of the unconscious. Beyond that, as we saw above, they take exactly the opposite view: we must inquire about meaning, but in a functional rather than semiotic sense. What we have to decipher is the social purpose behind the encoding of every aspect of daily life from the most mundane and the sheerly biological to the complex and metaphysical.

Anthropologists have of course been engaged in this task for a century or more, but mostly with a view to trying to understand what the codes mean to the people whose lives are structured by them. Deleuze and Guattari do not take this route. They aren't interested in 'local knowledge' or in finding out 'what natives think' (in Clifford Geertz's sense); rather what they are trying to discern is something on the order of the universal. By universal they mean non-psychological and indeed non-cultural. If a label has to be applied, then their choice would be 'machinic'. According to Deleuze and Guattari, Nietzsche rather than say Lévi-Strauss or Mauss, has provided the most important account of the anthropology of so-called primitive society. Nietzsche's thesis, which Deleuze and Guattari adopt and rewrite in their own language (to the point even of speaking for Nietzsche), is as follows: Man was constituted as a social being via the repression in himself of what Deleuze and Guattari refer to as either the 'germinal influx' or the 'biocosmic memory', by which they mean desire in its 'free labour' state, that is desire prior to 'primitive accumulation'.

All the stupidity and the arbitrariness of the laws, all the pain of the initiations, the whole perverse apparatus of repression and education, the red-hot irons, and the atrocious procedures have only this meaning: *to discipline* man [*dresser* l'homme], to mark him in his flesh, to render him capable of alliance, to form him within the debtor-creditor relation, which on both sides turns out to be a matter of memory – a memory straining toward the future. (AO, 207–8/225 translation modified)

Primitive rituals must suppress biological memory and transform it into memory for man written in words. If as Lacan argues the unconscious is structured like a language, then it is because of this process, which Deleuze and Guattari refer to as the 'system of cruelty' (after Nietzsche), and not a natural predisposition. The system of cruelty ensures that the organs are 'hewn into the socius' in such a way that 'man ceases to be a biological organism and becomes a full body, an earth, to which his organs become attached, where they are attracted, repelled, miraculated, following the requirements of a socius.' (AO, 159/169).

Primitive society is built on a foundation of collective ownership of all organs – by contrast, what we think of as postmodern or contemporary society effectively reverses this process, and by 'privatizing' the organs subordinates us to them (AO, 157/167). The collectively owned organs are referred to as the earth.

The earth is the primitive, savage unity of desire and production. For the earth is not merely the multiple and divided object of labour, it is also the unique, indivisible entity, the full body that falls back on the forces of production and appropriates them for its own as the natural or divine precondition. (AO, 154–5/164)

The earth is the body without organs on a social scale – it is in effect the body without organs of all the bodies without organs of all the individual subjects in any given society. Communities are formed in the same way as subjects: an aggregate of syntheses gives rise to a 'whole' that acts retroactively on the syntheses to yield an entity qualitatively different from its component parts. That entity is then enjoyed or consumed for itself. Deleuze and Guattari's thesis is that communities can be formed in this way because subjects are formed in this way. By the same token, subjects can be formed in this way because communities are. This is what is meant by their thesis that desire forms part of the infrastructure of society.

Social production, that is desire on a social scale, is not different in kind from desiring-production, indeed Deleuze and Guattari insist it is exactly the same as desiring-production, but determined by historical conditions that this chapter sets out to specify.

Desiring-production is also the limit of social production, it is what social production reverts to if its structures and mechanisms fail or are otherwise decomposed (e.g., schizophrenia). Social production functions in the same way as desiring-production: it has the same elements and the same processes; it differs only in modality (social production is molar whereas desiring-production is molecular – this is a difference in function not scale, the molar can reside in the individual just as the molecular can reside in the collective). It is on the surface of the earth that all the practices of inscription and consumption that taken together comprise what we call everyday life actually take place. Both the earth and the body without organs must be understood, then, as agents of repression.[54]

The territorial machine

Deleuze and Guattari's conception of the territorial machine overturns two paradigmatic assumptions that have conditioned the field of anthropology more or less since its inception: first, that the incest taboo is universal and proscribes a *real* desire; second, that all relations between subjects are ultimately relations of exchange. Deleuze and Guattari argue that neither of these hypotheses hold up under scrutiny. Their counterargument is that the incest taboo is an instrument of socialization that captivates desire by luring it into feeling guilty; and that society is inscriptive not exchangist.

So, how does the territorial machine work? First of all it has to capture desire and compel it to change function. There isn't a single or universal repressing agent, Deleuze and Guattari insist, but rather an affinity or co-efficiency between desiring-machines and social machines (AO, 201/217). The medium through which this affinity or co-efficiency works is the system of representation, which takes hold of and represses the 'germinal influx' that is desire's representative. The germinal influx refers to – that is, it presupposes – a flow that isn't codable. By codable Deleuze and Guattari mean capable of generating an 'equivalent' of some type, something that can *supplement* (in Derrida's sense) the original flow both in the sense of taking its place and of multiplying it.

For the flows to be codable, their energy must allow itself to be quantified and qualified; it is necessary that selections from the flows be made in relation to detachments from the chain: something must pass through but something must also be blocked, and something must block and cause to pass through. (AO, 178/192)

What passes through compensates for what is blocked, creating a surplus value of code which for Deleuze and Guattari is central to understanding desire (AO, 179/192–3). Coding is usually, though not exclusively, accomplished by means of prohibition and exclusion. The most well-known and indeed the most obviously significant example of this is the prohibition against incest. But as Deleuze and Guattari insist, incest is strictly speaking impossible and herein lays their practical dispute with psychoanalysis.

The possibility of incest [from the point of view of the unconscious] would require *both persons and names* – son, sister, mother, brother, father. Now in the incestuous act we can have persons at our disposal, but they lose their names inasmuch as these names are inseparable from the prohibition that proscribes them as partners; or else the names subsist, and designate nothing more than prepersonal intensive states that could just as well 'extend' to other persons, as when one calls his legitimate wife 'mama', or one's sister his wife. (AO, 177/190)

We can 'never enjoy the person and the name at the same time – yet this would be the condition for incest' (AO, 177/190). We can only understand this if we go back to the discussion of desiring-production and the legitimate and illegitimate uses of its syntheses. The system of persons corresponds to the illegitimate use of the syntheses of the unconscious; it renders subjects global and specific and institutes restrictive and segregative relations between them. By contrast, the system of names corresponds to the legitimate use of the syntheses of the unconscious and it is *this* that is truly desired.

What is desired is the intense germinal or germinative flow, where one would look in vain for persons or even functions discernible as father, mother, son, sister, etc., since these names only designate intensive variations on the full body of the earth determined as the germen. (AO, 177/191)

What the incest prohibition in fact proscribes then is uncoded desire; what the prohibition enacts is precisely a codification of desire.

There are three levels to this codification: 'Incest as it is prohibited (the form of discernible persons) is employed to repress incest as it is desired (the substance of the intense earth).' (AO, 178/191). Meanwhile the desire to transgress this prohibition, for which the figure of Oedipus is emblematic, is put forward as a lure to conceal the true form of desire. 'It matters little that this image is "impossible": it does its work from the moment that desire lets itself be caught as though by the impossible itself. You see, *that* is what you wanted!' (AO, 178/191). The three parts of the system then are: (1) germinal influx as the *representative of desire*; (2) the prohibition against this representative of desire is the *repressing representation*; (3) while the figure of the transgressor is the *displaced representative* (AO, 180–1/193).

> Incest is only the retroactive effect of the repressing representation *on* the repressed representative: the representation disfigures or displaces this representative against which it is directed; it projects onto the representative, categories, rendered discernible, that it has itself established; it applies to the representative terms that did not exist before the alliance organised the positive and the negative into a system in extension – the representation reduces the representative to what is blocked in the system. (AO, 181/195)

How does this work in practice? Consider for example the now largely obsolete prohibition on sex before marriage in Western societies. This prohibition depicted sex outside of the marriage as deleterious to the well-being of both the individual and society itself inasmuch as it was deemed to promote lasciviousness and a cavalier attitude towards relationships. But as is obvious enough, it is the prohibition itself that creates the possibility of 'sex before marriage', which in this sense is equivalent to incest. The point is that the very desire called 'sex before marriage' is created by the prohibition so as to be dishonoured, and does not in this sense represent real desire. It is a displacement of real desire which as Deleuze and Guattari tirelessly argue knows neither persons nor names. The supposed reward for respecting this prohibition was a happier, longer-lasting marriage and a stable society in which to bring up one's children. More particularly, respecting this code attracted prestige in the community, compensating for the loss of sexual freedom (libido is thus converted into numen and then voluptas). The logic behind this prohibition was extended to all aspects of daily life that might be construed as condoning lasciviousness – so, for instance, in the 1950s rock 'n' roll was subject to censorship. The length of skirts, the movement of hips when dancing, the style of music, were all seen as releasing undesirable flows of desire that had to be dammed up. Following Freud, Deleuze and Guattari refer to this process as secondary repression or repression proper (AO, 201/217). If this prohibition has fallen into a kind of moral redundancy it is perhaps because it is seen as a contributing cause to an even graver moral problem, 'extra-marital sex', inasmuch that by drastically restricting sexual freedom on one side of the marriage divide it leads to delinquency on the other side. But we have to be wary of such conclusions because this assumes that the prohibition is directed against an actual pre-existing desire when in reality it is the prohibition that makes it possible in the first place.

Coding desire is not enough by itself to produce an enduring social machine, however, it is merely the means. A change in the nature of the relations between individuals in a group is required for a social machine to come into being. There are two kinds of relationships between people in groups, according to Deleuze and Guattari: affiliations and alliances, the former is linear in composition (uniting father and son to form a lineage) while the latter is lateral (uniting brothers and cousins to form a tribe). The social machine mobilizes both types towards its own ends.

> The whole system evolves between two poles: that of fusion through opposition to other groups, and that of scission through the constant formation of lineages aspiring to independence, with capitalisation of alliances and filiation. [. . .] The segmentary territorial machine makes use of scission to exorcise fusion, and impedes the concentration of power by maintaining the organs of chieftainry in a relationship of impotence with the group. (AO, 167/179)

Rarely if ever mentioned in the secondary literature on Deleuze and Guattari, filiation and alliance are absolutely central to any understanding of the political dimension of their work.[55] Corresponding to the legitimate and illegitimate uses of the passive syntheses – filiation is by nature intensive, non-specific, inclusive or non-restrictive and polyvocal, while alliance is extensive, specific, exclusive or restrictive and segregative – filiation and alliance are 'like the two forms of a primitive capital: fixed capital or filiative stock, and circulating capital or mobile blocks of debt' (AO, 161/172). The chief is descended from a long line of chiefs and derives his right to rule from his lineage (fixed capital); but he could not rule effectively if he did not form and maintain alliances outside of his immediate family through elaborate feasts and gift-giving, if in other words he did not use his wealth to induce others to be in his debt (circulating capital). By this means the chief converts perishable wealth – e.g., food, skins and weapons – into imperishable prestige, namely the mandate to rule. This disequilibrium in the machine is fundamental to its operation (AO, 164–5/176).

In this system the negative that has constantly to be negated is the apparent positive of 'stock', that is to say accumulated wealth that if allowed to grow would become capital and thereby begin to unleash flows of its own, flows that would escape codification. All the variations on the potlatch rituals, some of which include the deliberate destruction of surplus food by fire or dispatch into the sea, are structured to achieve this goal of eliminating 'stock'. In doing so, the tribe puts itself in the debt of its neighbours and at the mercy of the elements, thereby ensuring by power of necessity that all members of the tribe work together to stave off starvation. Tribe members wear the signs of their tribe on their flesh in acknowledgement of this common cause and their individual indebtedness to the tribe for providing for them.

> It is not because everyone is suspected, in advance, of being a future bad debtor; the contrary would be closer to the truth. It is the bad debtor who must be understood as if the marks had not sufficiently 'taken' on him, as if he were or had been unmarked. He has merely widened, beyond the limits allowed, the gap that separated the voice of alliance and the body of affiliation, to such a degree that it is necessary to re-establish the equilibrium through an increase in pain. (AO, 208/225)

Primitive inscription is the instrument whereby the intensive filiative relations of lineage and descent are bonded with the extensive allying relations of the tribe. However, alliances do not derive from affiliations; on the contrary, they are designed to counter the concentrated power of affiliation. By the same token, alliances are not the product of exchanges – the chief doesn't exchange his wealth for allegiance; he must convert his wealth into allegiance. There is no general equivalence – such as one finds in the capitalist system of money – in the primitive economy which would enable exchange: in consequence, and quite deliberately, the giver must always give more than is strictly necessary so as to ensure indebtedness, but by the same token to prevent this from becoming an exchange the ritual of gift-giving makes the gift seem like a theft[56] (AO, 203/219). 'The problem [that the social machine must resolve] is one of passing from an intensive energetic order to an extensive system, which comprises both qualitative alliances and extended filiations.' (AO, 170/183). This is the purpose of primitive inscription.

Primitive inscription requires three things:

> a voice that speaks or intones, a sign marked in bare flesh, an eye that extracts enjoyment from the pain; these are the three sides of a savage triangle forming a territory of resonance and retention, a *theatre of cruelty* that implies the triple independence of the articulated voice, the graphic hand, and the appreciative eye. (AO, 207/224)

The voice is the voice of the alliance, the marked body is the body of affiliation, and the appreciative eye enables the declension of the two. Primitive inscription should not be confused with writing – indeed, Deleuze and Guattari go so far as to say it is writing's contrary (AO, 206/223).

> Savage formations are oral, are vocal, but not because they lack a graphic system: a dance on the earth, a drawing on the wall, a mark on the body are a graphic system, a geo-graphism, a geography. These formations are oral precisely because they possess a graphic system that is independent of the voice, a system that is not aligned on the voice and not subordinate to it, but connected to it, coordinated 'in an organisation that is radiating, as it were', and multidimensional. (AO, 206/222)

The tribal shaman, the one charged with the task of performing the inscription, does not *write* on the body – the tribespeople are not 'branded' in ritual in the sense of simply acquiring an identity mark that might perhaps be acquired by other less traumatic means.

Modern forms of so-called neo-tribalism, such as tattooing and body-piercing, is not in this respect properly tribal or ritualistic. It is both too aesthetic in its aims and too anaesthetic in its performance. The flesh must be torn – the rock mustn't be too sharp – and the pain witnessed for it is 'the terrible equivalence between the voice of alliance that inflicts and constrains, and the body afflicted by the sign that a hand is carving in it' that produces the desired result. Between the voice and the hand, 'pain is like the surplus value that the eye extracts, taking hold of the effect of active speech on the body, but also of the reaction of the body insofar as it is acted upon' (AO, 207/224). The resulting mark attaches a name to a person and by forcibly expelling the child from the world of the biocosmic creates a subject whose organs have been pledged to the collective.

The despotic machine

Who brought the primitive system to an end? 'Some pack of blond beasts of prey', as Nietzsche put it, meaning the founders of the state (AO, 209/227). The basic components of the despotic machine were always already present in the territorial machine, but ritual inoculated the socius against their toxic sting and prevented them from becoming organized in such a way as to become machinic in their own right. In this sense, it can even be said that the territorial machine presupposes the despotic machine (AO, 239/260). That is to say, it could not be haunted by what it could not imagine (even if it could not give a definite shape to its fears), thus it has to be said that the territorial machine knew about the despotic regime all along. The extension of this thesis, which is central to Deleuze and Guattari's account of the despotic regime, is that the state did not come into being piecemeal, or in stages, but was born fully formed. 'The State was not formed in progressive stages; it appears fully armed, a master stroke executed all at once; the primordial *Urstaat*, the eternal model of everything the State wants to be and desires.' (AO, 237/257). This is only possible – in both the theoretical and historical sense of that word, which is to say at once logical and realizable – because the despotic state knows only a virtual existence. The despotic machine is an abstraction that is only realized as an abstraction (AO, 240/261). In this way, it conditions both what came before and what followed, namely the primitive territorial machine and the modern capitalist machine. This is only logically and practically possible insofar as we conceive the despotic machine *dialectically* as a 'vanishing mediator' (to use Jameson's important concept, which I will explain in a moment).

Any doubt that we might have that this concept should be so understood – that it should be treated dialectically in other words – is dispelled by Deleuze and Guattari themselves when they cite Marx's concession in the introduction to the *Grundrisse* that it is possible, as Hegel insisted, for history to proceed from the abstract to the concrete (AO, 240–1/261). Marx generally took the view that Hegel got things back to front in this regard and famously described his own conception of the dialectic as a case of standing Hegel on his feet.[57] The one exception to this rule, however, is money:

> Money may exist, and did exist historically, before capital existed, before banks existed, before wage labour existed, etc. Thus in this respect it may be said that the simpler category can express the dominant relations of a less developed whole, or else those subordinate relations of a more developed whole which already had a historical existence before this whole developed in the direction expressed by a more concrete category. To that extent the path of abstract thought, rising from the simple to the combined, would correspond to the real historical process.[58]

Deleuze and Guattari argue that the concept of the state should be thought in exactly the same way:

> The State was first this abstract unity that integrated subaggregates functioning separately; it is now subordinated to a field of forces whose flows it coordinates and whose autonomous relations of domination and subordination it expresses. (AO, 241/261)

The crucial implication in all this is that the despotic machine has never *actually* existed. Its existence is, and has only ever been, virtual in nature. Therefore, our experience of the modern capitalist state in either the personal or the collective sense cannot be used to guide us in our understanding of the despotic machine. It does not function in the same way as its (never extant) predecessor. Indeed, its function is purely theoretical: it mediates between the primitive territorial machine and the modern capitalist machine. It is a passage that follows the path of the knight's move, zigzagging from its point of departure to its destination without stopping at any of the points in between. Given that the despotic machine remains abstract throughout this process, it can only be described as a 'vanishing mediator', that is to say a catalytic agent enabling the transmission of energies between different mutually incompatible social regimes.

> In theory the despotic barbarian formation has to be conceived of in terms of an opposition between it and the primitive territorial machine: the birth of an empire. But in reality one can perceive the movement of this formation just as well when one empire breaks away from a preceding empire; or even when there arises the dream of a spiritual empire, or wherever empires fall into decadence. (AO, 211/228)

Deleuze and Guattari insist that the despotic machine is not a transitional stage between the primitive and the modern, and indeed it could not be given its virtual status; but that doesn't stop it from being a mediator of the vanishing type.

> Such a picture of historical change – however irreconcilable it may be with vulgar Marxism – is in reality perfectly consistent with genuine Marxist thinking and is, indeed, at one with the model proposed by Marx himself for the revolutions of 1789 and 1848: in 1789 Jacobinism played the role of the vanishing mediator, functioning as the conscious and almost Calvinistic guardian of revolutionary morality, of bourgeois universalistic and democratic ideals, a guardianship that could be done away with in Thermidor, when the practical victory of the bourgeoisie was assured and an explicitly monetary and market system could come into being; and in that parody of 1789 which was the revolution of 1848, it was the similarly under the cloak of the traditions and values of the great revolution, and of the empire that followed it, that the new commercial society of the Second Empire emerged.[59]

So how does the despotic machine work? 'The founding of the despotic machine or the barbarian socius can be summarized in the following way: a new alliance and direct filiation. The despot challenges the lateral alliances and the extended filiations of the old community. He imposes a new alliance system and places himself in the direct filiation with the deity: the people must follow.' (AO, 210/228). The despot can be recognized by his willingness to start from zero, to scratch out everything that had gone before and begin again from a blank slate. Despotism is a form of social machine, rather than a particular psychological state, and although it can be the occasion of great violence, it need not manifest itself in a military operation. Moses, Saint-Paul, Saint-John, and even Christ, are for this reason counted among the despots according to Deleuze and Guattari, for what their visions entailed was precisely a new alliance with God based on a filiation proclaiming a chosen people, God's children (AO, 211/229). The despot, or his God, becomes the full body on which the socius inscribes itself, replacing the territorial machine's earth. However, what counts is not the person of the new sovereign, nor indeed his psychology, but the nature of the new regime this change inaugurates: the 'megamachine' of the state replaces the territorial machine, a new hierarchy is installed, placing the despot at the top and the villagers at the bottom, bureaucracy replaces intertribal alliance, and most importantly of all stock becomes the object of accumulation and correspondingly debt is rendered infinite in the form of tribute to the despot (AO, 212/230). 'What is suppressed is not the former *regime* of lateral alliances and extended filiations, but merely their determining character.' (AO, 213/231). The territorial machine's components continue to exist, but only as the cogs and wheels of the despotic machine that has overtaken them from within and without. The new regime overcodes all the previous codings of desire and in this way extracts its requisite share of surplus value.

As has already been signalled, the role of money is decisive in understanding the despotic machine. The despotic machine, like the primitive machine, feared the socially corrosive effects of decoded flows, particularly the flows of money its merchants unleashed. But having said that, money is the invention of the state, primarily for the purposes of taxation by means of which the state rendered debt infinite.

> The infinite creditor and infinite credit have replaced the blocks of mobile and finite debts. There is always a monotheism on the horizon of despotism: the debt becomes a *debt of existence*, a debt of the existence of the subjects themselves. A time will come

when the creditor has not yet lent while the debtor never quits repaying, for repaying is a duty but lending is an option. (AO, 215/234)

That time is now, as Deleuze would make explicit in his essay on the 'societies of control' (a nightmarish phrase he borrowed from William Burroughs): 'A man is no longer a man confined but a man in debt.' (N, 181/246). It is debt rather than the rule of law that holds the despotic machine together (AO, 216/235).

The implication of this statement, which in spite of appearances actually has more to do with how representation works than history, is probably not immediately obvious. It is, however, very clearly directed against the concept of the 'Law of the father' underpinning Lacan's psychoanalytically inflected semiotics (AO, 227/247). But also, and more explicitly, Derrida's grammatological semiotics, which does not draw a distinction between primitive inscription and what Deleuze and Guattari refer to as barbarian writing. Contrary to Derrida and indeed virtually the whole field of semiotics, with one or two noble exceptions, Deleuze and Guattari maintain that unlike the barbarian system of writing the primitive system of inscription does not consist of signs of signs, but positions of desire. In the despotic system, graphism aligns itself with the voice, inducing a new voice which speaks from on high. 'Then there occurs a crushing of the magic triangle: the voice no longer sings but dictates, decrees; the graphy no longer dances, it ceases to animate bodies, but is set to writing on tablets, stones, and books; the eye sets itself to reading.' (AO, 223/243). The crushing of the magic triangle gives rise to a mute voice that only expresses itself through writing, just as the Bible records: God laid down his laws at the same moment he ceased to speak directly to man.

Now the question of 'what does it mean?' becomes possible – and 'problems of exegesis prevail over problems of use and efficacy. The emperor, the god – what did he mean?' (AO, 224/243). It is our concern for this mysterious meaning from on high that subordinates us to the socius. We no longer require the mark of the socius in order to express our commitment to it, to make patent our pact with society. Henceforth writing can do nothing but bear witness to 'vanished despot' (AO, 225/245). There are two aspects to the becoming of the state: first it internalizes a field of increasingly decoded social forces (this could be said to constitute its physical system); second, it spiritualizes a supraterrestrial field which it overcodes (this could be said to constitute its metaphysical system). Translated, this means the state unleashes market forces (i.e., decoded flows), that exceed its grasp in all directions, its ability to overcode in other words, and this process eventually leads to an inversion of the relation between the sovereign and the system he heads. At the supreme point of the development of this process of inversion, the state is transformed into a mechanism of business. But even as its real power diminishes, the state reinvents itself as a 'moral authority'. Thus, as Deleuze and Guattari frequently say, what the state deterritorializes with one hand it reterritorializes with the other. It provides the moral glue that unites the axiomatic of capital with the assemblage of the people.

The civilized capitalist machine

But these decoded flows unleashed by the despotic machine are not by themselves enough to 'induce the birth of capitalism' (AO, 243/263). Capitalism does not begin, doesn't break free from the long period of latency that is the despotic age (which in this section Deleuze and Guattari start referring to by the more familiar name of 'Feudalism'), and come into being in its own right until the advent of the industrial revolution when it appropriates production itself.

> Doubtless the merchant was very early an active factor in pro-
> duction, either by turning into an industrialist himself in occu-
> pations based on commerce, or by making artisans into his own
> intermediaries or employees (the struggle against the guilds and
> the monopolies). But capitalism doesn't begin, the capitalist
> machine is not assembled, until capital directly appropriates pro-
> duction, and until financial capital and merchant capital are no
> longer anything but specific functions corresponding to a division
> of labour in the capitalist mode of production in general. (AO,
> 246/268)

This is the historical transformation for which Marx's general formula of capital MCM' was intended, the moment when capital begets capital, the moment when capital becomes filiative (AO, 247/269).

This is no longer the cruelty of life, the terror of one life brought to bear against another life [as was the case in the primitive territorial machine], but a *post-mortem* despotism, the despot become anus and vampire: 'Capital is dead labour, that vampire-like, only lives by sucking living labour, and lives the more, the more labour it sucks.' Industrial capital thus offers a new filiation that is a constituent part of the capitalist machine, in relation to which commercial capital and financial capital will now take the form of a new alliance by assuming specific functions. (AO, 248/270)

If one wants to understand how desire is induced, managed and channelled into socially sanctioned avenues, then one needs to understand how banking works, for it is banks that orchestrate this new arrangement of filiation and alliance. Indeed, Deleuze and Guattari will go so far as to say that if one wants to 'return to Marx' (in the manner of Lacan's famous 'return to Freud'), then one needs to return to his work on banking practice (AO, 250/273).

As Deleuze and Guattari insist throughout *Anti-Oedipus*, contradictions are not what bring social systems down; on the contrary, they are the very motors which give society its dynamism. Social machines feed off

the contradictions they give rise to, on the crises they provoke, on the anxieties they *engender*, and on the infernal operations they regenerate. Capitalism has learned this, and has ceased doubting itself, while even socialists have abandoned belief in the possibility of capitalism's natural death by attrition. (AO, 166/178)

The defining contradiction at the heart of the modern capitalist machine, the ultimate obscenity which it must constantly try to paper over, is the scandalous difference in kind between the money of the wage earner and the money of the financier, between money that functions purely as payment (alliance) and money that functions as finance (filiation).

In the one case, there are impotent money signs of exchange value, a flow of the means of payment relative to consumer goods and use values, and a one-to-one relation between money and an imposed range of products ('which I have a right to, which are my due, so they're mine'); in the other case, signs of the power of capital, flows of financing, a system of differential quotients of production that bear witness to a prospective force or to a long-term evaluation, not realisable *hic et nunc*, and functioning as an axiomatic of abstract quantities. (AO, 249/271)

The money in my pocket can be used to buy goods and even to set a value on certain goods, but ultimately this is a limited power in that its effects are always confined to an extremely localized sphere of influence. In contrast, the financier's money is capable of affecting the lives of millions, indeed billions, of people as is evident in the operations of the World Bank and the International Monetary Fund (IMF). These two institutions, supposedly disinterested and global in outlook, but in reality acting out US policy, transform the finances of whole nations into mere wage earner's payment money.[60] Persuaded that a First World standard of living is in reach, Third World nations have taken on vast amounts of debt in order to undertake a variety of infrastructure projects that have for the most part done little if anything to benefit the majority of citizens. That debt has meanwhile reduced them to a state of peonage as the interest payments required have sucked the life out of their national economies.[61]

The dream the Third World has been talked into adopting as its own is the dream of transforming payment money into finance money. No

integration of the dominated classes could occur without the shadow of this unapplied principle of convertibility – which is enough, however, to ensure that the Desire of the most disadvantaged creature will invest with all its strength, irrespective of any economic understanding or lack of it, the capitalist social field as a whole. (AO, 249–50/272)

Thus Deleuze and Guattari can say it is the banks that control desire in contemporary society. This is no less true today than it was in 1972, when *Anti-Oedipus* was published; indeed it is no exaggeration to say that it is truer today than it was then.[62]

Measuring the two orders of magnitude [i.e., the two types of money] in terms of the same analytic unit is a pure fiction, a cosmic swindle, as if one were to measure intergalactic or intra-atomic distances in metres and centimetres. There is no common measure between the value of the enterprises and that of the labour capacity of wage earners. (AO, 250/273)

As Michael Parenti argues, terms like 'development' (as found in such bureaucratic buzz-words like 'community development' or 'developing world') are mobilized to disguise precisely this fact. Contemporary cultural studies' refusal of such labels as 'First World' and 'Third World', allegedly on the grounds that such terms are elitist, cannot but be seen as complicit, albeit unwittingly, with the present order of things known as the 'Washington Consensus'.[63]

This dualism at the heart of the capitalist system has its own inner dynamic which Marx himself diagnozed as the tendency towards a falling rate of profit. Capitalist investment is constantly coming up against this problem. No matter how profitable an investment initially is, the rate of profit-making inevitably declines over time. In a housing boom, to take a relatively simple example, prices might rise by as much as 100 per cent in the space of a year, effectively doubling the cost of houses, which is an astonishing rate of profit-making. If a house cost $100,000 at the start of the year, it would be worth $200,000 by the year's end. If the same rate of profit-making were to continue, it would be worth $400,000 at the end of the second year, and so on. Tied as it is to a host of external factors, including the cost of borrowing money, the relative cost of real estate elsewhere, the real growth in wages, and so on, this rate of profit-making rarely lasts more than a year or so in the housing market, which is why such moments are referred to as 'booms'. They are short-lasting and powerful in effect, but ultimately unsustainable. Smart property investors know this and are constantly on the look-out for the next boom as a way of maintaining the rate of profit-making. On a larger scale, manufacturing has been exported from the First World to the Third World for the same reason: *to maintain the rate of profit*. It is much cheaper to manufacture goods in the low wage regions of the Third World, but those cost savings are rarely passed onto the consumer. More usually they are passed directly to the company directors and shareholders in the form of dividends and an enhanced capitalization of their stock. The tendency towards a falling rate of profit is a continually recurring 'crisis' for capitalism, but not one it has any interest in overcoming. In fact, it is the principal motor powering the system, giving it its restless energy. This is what Deleuze and Guattari mean when they say the system only works by breaking down.

If capitalism is the exterior limit of all societies [as was argued above in relation to the primitive territorial machine and the despotic machine], this is because capitalism for its part has no exterior limit, but only an interior limit that is capital itself and that it does not encounter, but reproduces by always displacing it. (AO, 251/274)

Capitalism thrives on its own self-induced crises. Deleuze and Guattari describe this process as 'schizophrenization', whereby capitalism displaces its crisis of accumulation from the centre to the periphery and back again. This process, also known as the 'development of underdevelopment', enables the centre to maintain its rate of profit, viewed from the global perspective of capitalism itself, but leads to the destruction of local industry (all sectors – primary, secondary and tertiary) in the periphery (AO, 254/277). But in spite of its willingness to change, even if that means destroying tradition, capitalism is essentially conservative in its outlook. It only embraces innovation when it is profitable to do so. 'In general, the introduction of innovations always tends to be delayed beyond the time scientifically necessary, until the moment when the market forecasts justify their exploitation on a large scale.' (AO, 254/277). That this is true can readily be seen in the criminally sluggish response by governments to the threat of climate change, particularly in those countries who are among the worst offenders such as the US and Australia. In a way, it compels us to accept the neo-liberal dictum that the only solution to the problem of global warming is a market solution, however distasteful that might be to some (including myself, I might add), because capitalist society only responds to the opportunity to make a profit.

If government can make environmentally responsible business practice profitable, then business will willingly embrace it. This is the thinking behind the 'cap and trade' model the European Union has adopted for carbon outputs: it requires businesses to reduce their carbon emissions by allocating an emissions quota, but also allows businesses to sell any surplus in their quota they might obtain through efficiency. In this way, as more than a few commentators have already complained, government has effectively given businesses in Europe a new and potentially valuable asset for free. The upside, it is hoped, is that now businesses have been given a powerful incentive to voluntarily reduce emissions they will adopt a greener attitude as making good business sense. Time will tell if this strategy works. It has worked in the case of sulphur emissions in the US, where a similar model was put in place a decade ago. What this means, however, is that the role of the state has dramatically changed from the despotic era: it no longer absorbs surplus value, but adds to it by creating the conditions in which capitalism thrives (AO, 255/278).[64]

But it is not even the economic changes capitalism entails that is decisive as far as Deleuze and Guattari are concerned. It is rather the nature of the social machine it produces that it is crucial. It has two main characteristics, which at first glance might appear contradictory: on the one hand, it stimulates (over-)production via a radical process of decoding; but on the other hand it retards that production by insinuating anti-production into every level of society. As we have seen, the primitive territorial machine established the social unit by coding the flows of desire, by giving them a meaning; the despotic machine loosened these codes up, but also bonded them to its own regime by overcoding them. It emptied the codes of their sacred content and at the same time spiritualized them, making them part of what defined 'good society'. Thus to use our previous example, if sex before marriage was prohibited in primitive society because it offended the gods, then in the despotic regime it was prohibited because it threatened the smooth transfer of capital (e.g., children born out of wedlock could not inherit property).

Capitalist decoding evacuates the meaning out of all codes, that is to say all the rules, regulations, laws, codes of conduct, and so forth, rendering them completely arbitrary, or rather purely functional. Decoding in this context doesn't mean interpretation or deciphering, it literally means taking the code away. Taking their place is the axiomatic.[65] 'Why not merely say that capitalism replaces one code with another, that it carries into effect a new type of coding?' (AO, 268/294). Because the axiomatic is different in kind to the code; it is unavowable:

> there is not a single economic or financial operation that, assuming it is translated in terms of code, would not lay bare its own unavowable nature, that is, its intrinsic perversion or essential cynicism (the age of bad conscience is also the age of pure cynicism). (AO, 268/294)

Capitalism is not something we can believe in – not even those free marketers who profess to 'believe' in the market actually do, otherwise they would not also demand its regulation. The US demands free access to global markets, but does not reciprocate: its markets are tightly controlled. But having said that, capitalism's flows aren't codeable: money is a general equivalent giving common measure to all things, but in itself floats free of all attempts to give it meaning (such as the gold standard that once served to guarantee currency) (AO, 269–70/294).

Capitalism doesn't require our belief to function, but it does require regulation. It unleashes flows that need damping if they aren't to carry the system itself into ruin. It needs to produce anti-production as well as production. The drive to innovation needs to be countered by the manufacture of stupidity. 'The State, its police, and its army form a gigantic enterprise of anti-production, but at the heart of production itself, and conditioning this production.' (AO, 256/280). The apparatus of anti-production serves two key functions:

> On the one hand, it alone is capable of realising capitalism's supreme goal, which is to produce in the large aggregates, to introduce lack where there is always too much, by effecting the absorption of overabundant resources. On the other hand, it alone doubles the capital and the flow of knowledge with a capital and an equivalent flow of *stupidity* [*connerie*] that also effects an absorption and a realisation, and that ensures the integration of groups and individuals into the system. (AO, 256/280)

Deleuze and Guattari have in mind what is sometimes referred to as 'military-Keynesianism', the process whereby governments use investment in military infrastructure as a mainstay of the economy. No government practises 'military-Keynesianism' more than the US, despite its constant anti-government spending rhetoric. The fact is the US government spends the equivalent of the entire GDP of India on its military and still worries that it hasn't spent enough. The statistics on military expenditure are nothing less than mind-boggling, but just to give one example that will speak directly to the point of the manufacture of stupidity: it is estimated that the cost of one fighter jet, an FA-18, say, which can cost upwards of $US300 million, would be sufficient to put 5,000 people through university. The infamous stealth bombers cost several times that figure. Meanwhile higher education in the US is becoming increasingly expensive and further and further beyond the reach of all but the wealthy few. But Deleuze and Guattari don't just mean these are stupid choices for a government to make, though undoubtedly they wouldn't disagree on that score; rather, by stupidity they mean the manufacture of consent, the constant flow of 'reasons to believe in this world' (to adapt a phrase from Deleuze's books on cinema). Ultimately this takes the form of a substitution of economics for politics. As Rancière argues, 'economic necessity', the catch cry of all governments in the postmodern era, is an extremely powerful depoliticizing card for politics to play.[66] No one has understood Althusser's dictum that the economic is the ultimately determining agency better than the neo-liberals, who have turned it into the source of their political legitimacy (their body without organs in other words).

> Marx often alluded to the Golden Age of the capitalist, when the latter didn't hide his own cynicism: in the beginning, at least, he could not be unaware of what he was doing, extorting surplus value. But how this cynicism has grown – to the point where he is able to declare: no, nobody is being robbed! (AO, 259/284)

This brings us to a second Marxian law adopted by Deleuze and Guattari in addition to the tendency towards a falling rate of profit and that is its complement: the law of the counteracted tendency.

> [Capitalism is] the limit of all societies, insofar as it brings about the decoding of the flows that the other social formations coded and overcoded. But it is the *relative* limit of every society; it effects *relative* breaks, because it substitutes for the codes an extremely rigorous axiomatic that maintains the energy of the flows in a bound state on the body of capital as a socius that is deterritorialised, but also a socius that is even more pitiless than any other. (AO, 267/292)

Schizophrenia is the true, or *absolute*, limit of society, inasmuch that as we have seen what it brings about is a generalized freeing of all the flows of desire.

> Hence one can say that schizophrenia is the *exterior* limit of capitalism itself or the conclusion of its deepest tendency, but that

capitalism only functions on condition that it inhibit this tendency, or that it push it back or displace this limit, by substituting for its own *immanent* relative limits, which it continually reproduces on a widened scale. It axiomatises with one hand what it decodes with the other. Such is the way one must reinterpret the Marxist law of the counteracting tendency. (AO, 267/292)

Today, this is the role assigned to religions and traditions: the absorption of the deracinated energies capitalism has detached from its body. This is what Deleuze and Guattari mean by reterritorialization: the tying back down of desire. Consider the recent controversy in France over the right of Muslim girls to wear a *foulard* (head scarf) to school. Here the issue is not so much why the French government wanted to ban it, since that is fairly obvious – it made good political sense to do so (in Le Pen's case it was nearly enough to win him the Presidency) – but why the girls should want to wear them in the first place given that in France there is no requirement to do so. Indeed, in 2003, out of approximately 250,000 Muslim schoolgirls in France it was estimated that only 1,200 actually wore a *foulard* with any regularity. One obvious explanation for their decision to wear the scarf in spite of the freedom not to do so is that it enables them to construct a Muslim identity as a means of negotiating a space for themselves in a culture that isn't their own.[67] Far from being coerced into wearing the *foulard*, far from it being a sign of their oppression by a patriarchal doctrine as many French feminists argued, Muslim schoolgirls chose to do so because it was empowering. The *foulard* is a 'neoterritoriality', an archaism with a perfectly modern function (AO, 279/306).

Modern societies are caught between two poles.

Born of decoding and deterritorialisation, on the ruins of the despotic machine, these societies are caught between the Urstaat that they would like to resuscitate as an overcoding and reterritorialising unity, and the unfettered flows that carry them toward an absolute threshold. (AO, 282/309)

In effect, modern societies are torn in two directions: 'archaism and futurism, neoarchaism and ex-futurism, paranoia and schizophrenia' (AO, 282/309–10). What is crucial to understand in all this is that the relations of alliance and filiation which structure all types of

DELEUZE AND GUATTARI'S *ANTI-OEDIPUS*

society no longer apply to people, as they did in the previous territorial and despotic regimes. In the modern state, these relations apply to money. In this situation, 'the family becomes a microcosm, suited to expressing what it no longer dominates' (AO, 286/315). The family becomes an object of consumption in the modern system. It is on this terrain that Oedipus can finally take root. 'The Oedipal triangle is the personal and private territoriality that corresponds to all of capitalism's efforts at social reterritorialisation.' (AO, 289/317). Its purpose is to neutralize the threat of schizophrenia, the modern capitalist machine's absolute limit, by creating an *interior* limit to the movement of desire that pulls it up short of the *exterior* limit (i.e., schizophrenia).

INTRODUCTION TO SCHIZOANALYSIS

A little additional effort is enough to overturn everything, and to lead us finally toward other far-off places.
                              Gilles Deleuze and Félix Guattari, *Anti-Oedipus*

Schizoanalysis has one single aim – to get revolutionary, artistic, and analytic machines working as parts, cogs, of one another.
                              Gilles Deleuze, *Negotiations*

So, what is the revolutionary path? What is the solution?

Is there one? – To withdraw from the world market, as Samir Amin advises Third World countries to do, in a curious revival of the fascist 'economic solution'? Or might it be to go in the opposite direction? To go still further, that is, in the movement of the market, of decoding and deterritorialisation? (AO, 260/285)

Perhaps we haven't gone far enough? Perhaps the means to bringing about the end of the present system lies within it?[68] Psychoanalysis is no help in sorting this question out, Deleuze and Guattari argue, because it is already part of the very social system they aim to critique. So what does schizoanalysis propose? Deleuze and Guattari do not offer a model that we can follow if we want to be revolutionaries. They do, however, outline three tasks – one negative and two positive – that will better position us to become revolutionaries, should we choose to go down that path, by arming us against the many betrayals all revolutions seem to suffer, namely the betrayals that come from within. *Anti-Oedipus* is not so much pro-revolution as it is anti-counterrevolution. The fascist inside that Foucault warns us against in his preface is precisely the counterrevolutionary, the revolutionary who has lost their faith in the revolution, the courage of their convictions, and the will to change. In this sense, *Anti-Oedipus* is a polemic against both the cynicism of the right and the defeatism of the left.

The negative task

'Destroy, destroy. The task of schizoanalysis goes by way of destruction – a whole scouring of the unconscious, a complete curettage.' (AO, 342/371). What must be destroyed? Oedipus, the ego, the superego, guilt, law, castration, all these things must be rooted out at the source. It isn't simply a matter of 'working through' these things, either, as one does in psychoanalysis, since this only destroys something the better to conserve it. In psychoanalysis we 'work through' our guilt not to get rid of it, but to own to it, to internalize it all the more. We overcome our castration anxiety so as to reach the point of resignation and acceptance psychoanalysis demands of us. Identifying with our symptoms, as the Lacanians demand, is not the same thing as extinguishing the cause of the symptoms, namely, guilt, law and castration. Getting rid of Oedipus in this sense simply means turning it into an idea, which is in fact its most toxic form. 'Only the idea can inject venom.' (AO, 343/372). The destruction process Deleuze and Guattari have in mind is much more thoroughgoing in purpose and effect than anything contemplated by psychoanalysis. As we've seen already, getting rid of Oedipus for Deleuze and Guattari means getting rid of it both as a problem and a solution. Thus one can neither retreat to a pre-Oedipal phase nor project a post-Oedipal phase as a means of escaping the Oedipal trap. Ultimately what's at stake is the rediscovery of the anOedipal operation of desire behind and beneath Oedipal representations. Destruction is essentially a practical matter of undoing the complex set of illusions (i.e., territories in Deleuze and Guattari's terms) by means of which we give structure and purpose to our lives. But it also entails a politics. Perhaps it should be said that the only effective politics is a practical one – this would be the meaning then of 'practical Deleuzism', the watchword of this project. That is certainly the approach Deleuze and Guattari take.

In agreement with psychoanalysis, Deleuze and Guattari take the view that

> unconscious representations can never be apprehended independently of the deformations, disguises, or displacements it undergoes. Unconscious representation therefore comprises essentially, by virtue of its own *law*, a represented that is displaced in relation to an agency in a constant state of displacement. (AO, 344/373)

But, they say, psychoanalysis draws two false conclusions from this initial premise. First, that the agency in question can be discerned on the flipside of the displaced represented; and second, that this agency is a nonrepresented representative (or 'lack') obtruding in the sphere of representation. For Deleuze and Guattari, the *locus classicus* of this particular error is the assumption that one can deduce the nature of desire from what is prohibited. As we saw in the case of incest (see previous section), the prohibition is a way of dishonouring desire, a way of trapping it with a false image.

> Oedipus is indeed the displaced represented; yes, castration is indeed the representative, the displacing agency (*le déplaçant*), the signifier – but none of that constitutes an unconscious material, nor does any of it concern the productions of the unconscious. Oedipus, castration, the signifier, etc., exist at the crossroads of two operations of capture: one where repressive social production becomes replaced by beliefs, the other where repressed desiring-production finds itself replaced by representations. (AO, 345/374)

It is this operation of capture that needs to be understood if an effective 'cure' is to be carried out, one that actually extinguishes the cause of particular symptoms. That psychoanalysis goes about this in the wrong way is obvious, Deleuze and Guattari argue, from the fact that the peculiarly pernicious effect of the so-called psychoanalytic cure is that it preserves the very thing it is supposed to get rid of: it causes repudiated beliefs to survive and unbelievers to believe, by creating 'a private territory for them' (AO, 345/374).

> That is why, inversely, schizoanalysis must devote itself with all its strength to the necessary destructions. Destroying beliefs and

representations, theatrical scenes. And when engaged in this task no activity will be too malevolent. (AO, 345/374)

The complication in all this is the fact that it is indeed necessary 'for desiring-production to be induced from representation, to be discovered through its lines of escape [*lignes de fuite*]' (AO, 346/375). Given a certain effect, what machine could have produced it? This is the basic question we have been taught to ask. We have also been taught to assume that the machine producing certain effects function differently from how they are formed. The contrast with psychoanalysis is obvious. Thus there is no simple path from an effect back to its ultimate cause. And as we've seen, all the many conceptual inventions of *Anti-Oedipus* are needed precisely to solve the analytic problem presented by this very fact. Here, though, Deleuze and Guattari show that it is the concepts of deterritorialization and reterritorialization that offer the most effective tools for this purpose. The basic premise of this pair of concepts is this: 'The movement of deterritorialisation can never be grasped in itself, one can only grasp its indices in relation to the territorial representations.' (AO, 347/377). These indices are desiring-machines, which can take a variety of forms – an airplane, a train, a bicycle, sewing machine, or whatever. The one caveat is that it must not be a person. 'Psychoanalysis, with its Oedipal stubbornness, has only a dim understanding of this; for one reterritorialises on persons and surroundings, but one deterritorialises on machines.' (AO, 348/378).

Take for example André Brink's post-apartheid novel *The Rights of Desire*. The main protagonist and narrator, Ruben Olivier, a retired librarian in his sixties, falls in love with a young woman, Tessa Butler, who rents out his spare room. The path of their love is not smooth. She agrees to love him only on condition that they do not sleep together. Nonetheless she allows him to see her naked and he is captivated by her navel ring. On his birthday, she gives him the navel ring and he treasures it, telling himself everything will be alright in the world so long as he has this. Predictably he loses it and his relationship with Tessa comes to an end, though not for that reason. Once Tessa leaves him he suddenly rediscovers the ring and once again he feels that everything is alright with his world. But he also notices that his world is changed; he longs to see what's outside the confines of his big house in the suburbs where has exiled himself for the past decade or more. It is tempting to say that Brink must

have read his Deleuze, to speak like Žižek, because the reason Ruben
and Tessa break up is precisely that they recognize that their relationship is born of addiction: each is reterritorializing on the other
– she needs a father figure (perhaps) and he needs a second chance
with his deceased wife (perhaps), but either way their relationship
isn't healthy. It's too theatrical and they eventually realize it. But
even so, their coming together disrupts the little territories they'd
each carved out for themselves, sending them both on schizo
voyages. Pondering what it means to him to have known and lost
Tessa, Ruben concludes: 'I am alone now, in this tumultuous desert
where Tessa has left me after disrupting the flatness of my old world.
But I am also not alone.'[69] Humming in the middle of that desert is
the little navel ring which he keeps close.

The principal destructive task is the elimination of reterritorialization – Deleuze and Guattari depict reterritorialization as a constant threat.

> Even those who are best at 'leaving' [i.e., deterritorializing], those
> who make leaving into something as natural as being born or
> dying, those who set out in search of nonhuman sex – Lawrence,
> Miller – stake out a far-off territoriality that still forms an anthro-
> pomorphic and phallic representation: the Orient, Mexico, or
> Peru. Even the schizo's stroll or voyage does not effect great deter-
> ritorialisations without borrowing from territorial circuits: the
> tottering walk of Molloy and his bicycle preserves his mother's
> room as the vestige of a goal and so on. (AO, 346–7/376)

Our territories are our addictions, our perversions. Perversion
for Deleuze and Guattari is simply reterritorialization by another
name; it

> comprises all the types of reterritorialisations, not merely artifi-
> cial, but also exotic, archaic, residual, private, etc.: thus Oedipus
> and psychoanalysis as perversion. Even Raymond Roussel's
> schizophrenic machines turn into perverse machines in the
> theatre representing Africa. (AO, 347/377)

Undoubtedly the same could be said for the other machines we've
encountered – not just Beckett's and Roussel's, but also Artaud's,
Büchner's and Schreber's. Doubtless, too, Ruben's little navel ring

with its blood red jewel is a perverse machine too. 'In short, there is no deterritorialisation of the flows of schizophrenic desire that is not accompanied by global or local reterritorialisations, reterritorial-isations that always reconstitute shores of representation.' (AO, 347/377). That is to say, if we can ask the question 'what does it mean?', then we are dealing with a reterritorialization and we'll know we've undone it when that question ceases to be possible all over again.

> In each case we must go back by way of old lands [i.e., past reter-ritorializations and their resultant territories], study their nature, their density; we must seek to discover how the machinic indices are grouped on each of these lands that permit going beyond them. How can we reconquer the process each time, constantly resuming the journey on these lands – Oedipal lands of neurosis, artificial lands of perversion, clinical lands of psychosis? (AO, 350/380)

The answer to this last question is simply this: the negative task of undoing reterritorilizations must always be accompanied by the pos-itive task of understanding how and why those reterritorializations were constructed in the first place. Deleuze and Guattari place a great premium on self-knowledge – but rather than asking us to get to know our inner self, they require us to come to know how that inner self was constituted.

First positive task

'The first positive task consists of discovering in a subject the nature, the formation, or the functioning of *his* desiring-machines, inde-pendently of any interpretations. What are your desiring-machines, what do you put into these machines, what is the output, how does it work, what are your nonhuman sexes?' (AO, 354/384). In order to reach the point of being able to answer these questions the investi-gation must push beyond the interpretative realm – the realm in which the question 'what does it mean?' still applies – into what Deleuze and Guattari specify as the functional or machinic realm. This is the case for all the machines – social, technical and desiring – with which we fabricate our lives. Deleuze and Guattari adapt the following rule for recognizing the parts of machines from Lacanian psychoanalyst Serge Leclaire:

the elements or parts of the desiring-machines are recognised by their mutual independence, such that nothing in the one depends or should depend on something in the other. They must not be opposed determinations of the same entity, nor the differentiations of a single being, such as the masculine and feminine in the human sex, but different or really-distinct things (*des réellement-distincts*), distinct 'beings', as found in the dispersion of the nonhuman sex (the clover and the bee). (AO, 355–6/386)

Unless schizoanalysis arrives at these dispersed elements of what Leclaire referred to as the 'erogenous body', by which he meant something of the order of what Deleuze and Guattari themselves refer to as 'singularities' or 'intensities', that is, pre-personal, pre-individual, pre-subjective, libidinally charged particles, then it hasn't taken things far enough. Putting it more simply, it is a matter of unearthing those particles that have been assembled, brought into a relation of connection, disjunction and conjunction, in the absence of an overarching link or external framing device, such as the phallus or the organism.

It is true that one might instead wonder how these conditions of dispersion, of real distinction, and of the absence of a link permit any machinic *regime* to exist – how the partial objects thus defined are able to form machines and arrangements of machines. The answer lies in the passive nature of the syntheses, or – what amounts to the same thing – in the indirect nature of the interactions under consideration. (AO, 357/387–8)

The 'true activities of the unconscious, causing to flow and breaking flows, consist of the passive synthesis itself insofar as it ensures the relative coexistence and displacement of the two different functions' (AO, 357/388). Partial objects and the desiring-machines that mobilize them are the machinic components of the unconscious. As we have seen, these machinic components are blocked in their operation by a variety of different agents of repression – there is the body without organs itself, which corresponds to what psychoanalysis refers to as 'primary repression', then there are mechanisms of society itself, which correspond to what psychoanalysis calls 'secondary repression' or 'repression proper'. The particular problem here, as Deleuze and Guattari point out, is that the latter relies on the former: thus the first essential task of schizoanalysis is to disrupt the coincidence of the two, thus denying primary repression its reinforcement in the form of secondary repression and secondary repression its justification in the form of primary repression. Having done that, the schizoanalyst has to retool the relations of attraction and repulsion that characterize the union of primary and secondary repression in such a way as to enable the unconscious to become productive again. By this means it enables desiring-machines to renew their operation.

Second positive task

The second positive task of schizoanalysis consists of reaching

the investments of unconscious desire of the social field, insofar as they are differentiated from the preconscious investments of interest, and insofar as they are not merely capable of counteracting them, but also of coexisting with them in opposite modes. (AO, 383/419)

What do they mean by this? Deleuze and Guattari give the example of what they refer to as a 'generation gap' conflict between old people who reproach the young 'for putting their desires (a car, credit, a loan, girl-boy relationships) ahead of their interests (work, savings, a good marriage)' (AO, 384/419). They suggest that the problem here is that what is depicted as 'raw desire' – the desire to own a car, or obtain a credit card, and so on – is already a mixture of desire and interest, 'a mixture of forms of desire and of interest that are specifically reactionary and vaguely revolutionary' (AO, 384/419). In their own words, the situation is completely 'muddled'. The question this begs, of course, is how to unmuddle things, and thus fulfil the second task they've put before us. Their answer is that schizoanalysis has to use sexuality as an index of the state of things. But, and this is the real point of this section of *Anti-Oedipus*, this will not work so 'long as sexuality is kept – consciously or not – within narcissistic, Oedipal, and castrating coordinates that are enough to ensure the triumph of the most rigorous censors, the gray gentlemen mentioned by Lawrence' (AO, 384–5/420). So unmuddling the tangle of desire and interests means separating real, machinic desire from it's familialist and masturbatory other, namely fantasy.

For example, no 'gay liberation movement' is possible as long as homosexuality is caught up in a relation of exclusive disjunction with heterosexuality, a relation that ascribes them both to a common Oedipal and castrating stock, charged with ensuring only their differentiation in two noncommunicating series, instead of bringing to light their reciprocal inclusion and their transverse communication in the decoded flows of desire (included disjunctions, local connections, nomadic conjunctions). (AO, 384/420)

Sexuality cannot be liberated if it does not first of all dismantle the mechanism of sexual difference. Deleuze and Guattari's position regarding sexuality is radical in its simplicity. Sexual difference would not exist, they argue, if it did not serve the interest of power. Culturally we only observe and indeed obsess about the biological differences between the sexes because it is in our social interest to do so. Sexual difference is a means by which power exerts itself. The point is that sexual liberation, whether of women or men, or homosexuals, transsexuals, and so on, is not achieved by extending 'rights' of enjoyment to all interested parties, but by working to extinguish the factor of interest altogether. One has to get rid of both the problem and the solution.

Schizoanalysis is the variable analysis of the *n* sexes in a subject, beyond the anthropomorphic representation that society imposes on this subject, and with which it represents its own sexuality. The schizoanalytic slogan of the desiring-revolution will be first of all: to each its own sexes. (AO, 325/352)

Four theses

Anti-Oedipus concludes by mapping out four theses that in sum characterize the schizoanalytic project as a whole:

1. Every libidinal investment of the unconscious is social and bears upon a sociohistorical field (AO, 375/409).
2. There are two types of social investments: there is the unconscious libidinal investment of the group or desire and the preconscious investment of class or interest (AO, 377/411).
3. The non-familial libidinal investments of the unconscious have primacy over the familial investments of the unconscious (AO, 390/427).

4. The unconscious social investments of desire can be of two main types: paranoid, reactionary and fascisizing or schizoid, revolutionary and utopian (AO, 401/439).

In a very provisional fashion, we can get a sense of what a full-scale schizoanalysis of the contemporary cultural and political scene would amount to by using these four theses as the basic framework for a reading of Tom Frank's bestselling and highly persuasive account of the becoming-conservative of the US, *What's the Matter with Kansas?* Appearing shortly before the 2004 US federal election, Frank's book accurately predicted the swerve to the right that returned George W. Bush to the White House for a second term. As the first opportunity for the American people to rid themselves of the hawkish Bush II regime, this election was effectively a plebiscite on the 'War on Terror', or more particularly the conduct of US imperialism. The electorate had before them what to an outsider's eyes (given the US's global role, I agree with those critics who have suggested the rest of the world should be allowed to vote in US elections) appeared to be all the evidence needed to persuade them to get rid of Bush II: several thousand American troops had already been killed or wounded in Iraq, the Abu-ghraib scandal had already broken and the brutality of the incumbent's policies were there for all Americans to see, if they cared to look. The US economy was faltering – unemployment was rising, the dollar falling, the deficit ballooning, and welfare spending shrinking – and the homeland was anything but safe. Despite that, the Bush II regime was returned, admittedly not by a large margin and not without the aid of some very dodgy ballots, particularly in the all important swing-state of Ohio.[70] All of which suggests that if the electorate wasn't cynical before the election, they were bound to become so following it.

In such a context, one can have no difficulty understanding Slavoj Žižek's recent theoretical move to make cynicism the cornerstone of his analysis of the contemporary political situation, both as the essential problem to be confronted – or, rather, overcome – by any political group with the intention of changing society; and, as the definitive answer to the theoretical and sociological question of why the present political situation appears so confused and ultimately why radical change is seemingly so impossible. For him the problem is pervasive because its core attitude – encapsulated in the phrase he borrows from Octave Mannoni: 'Je sais bien, mais quand même . . .' ('I know very well, but all the same . . .') – forms the basis of *all* social and cultural behaviour, not only that which entails some kind of morally suspect action.[71] He doesn't say that we are all cynics, but he does suggest that our normal mode of being in the world requires us to disavow knowledge and this renders us susceptible to a cynical outlook. Žižek has countless examples of the everyday disavowal of knowledge he can point to in support of his argument: I know that the paper money in my wallet is really worthless, but all the same I act as though it is not; I know Santa doesn't really exist, but all the same I act as though he does; I have no way of knowing if my bank details really are secure, but all the same I act as though they are. Adapting Donald Rumsfeld in an essay on the Abu-ghraib scandal, Žižek referred to this disavowed knowledge as 'the "unknown knowns", things we don't know that we know, which is precisely the Freudian unconscious, the "knowledge which doesn't know itself", as Lacan used to say'.[72]

Ideology, for Žižek, is essentially a dual process of disavowing what one knows while reifying a false corollary (or to put it in the language of political spin-doctoring, 'bait and switch') – I know there are no Weapons of Mass Destruction in Iraq, but all the same Saddam Hussein is a terrible dictator who should be deposed. When it is put this way, cynicism does indeed seem to explain a great deal that is perplexing about the ideological make-up of contemporary society. How else can we explain the baffling lack of incredulity of Bush II's supporters? Conceptually, however, cynicism is subject to a law of diminishing returns. Its very premise – that 'I know very well . . .' – is empirically insupportable. In 2004 Bush II supporters did not appear to 'know very well' what he was likely to do as President. Certainly in 2000 they couldn't have known he would embroil them in two unwinnable wars, ransack environmental protection laws, stretch the national deficit to unprecedentedly high levels, or any of the other infelicitous acts he has performed since assuming office. In 2004, when this was known, did voters in Kansas, the subject of Tom Frank's book, know or believe that any of these acts were wrong? Did they, along with voters elsewhere in formerly blue but now staunchly red states, knowingly vote to continue with the two unwinnable wars, the ransacking of environmental protection laws, the stretching of the national deficit to even higher levels? Or, did they vote for Bush II hoping he would reverse things? And isn't it possible that voters balanced the issues out in a pragmatic fashion, reasoning for themselves that although Bush II had gotten them into the war, for which they'd like to vote against him, in all probability he is the best one to see them through it and therefore they had to vote for him? Is such a calculation cynical?

To speak of a 'they' in this context is obviously an analytic fiction – the 'they' here, to speak only of the US election in question, comprises hundreds of millions of people, not all of whom actually voted. In fact, the non-voters vastly exceeded the voters, raising a whole other set of questions about whether it is more or less cynical, to give only one frame to it, to abstain from voting. These are obviously volatile issues and for good reason Tom Frank doesn't engage with them. His focus is the much more down to earth and ultimately much more self-interested issue of labour. We might ask, then, did Kansas's voters know in 2004 that the Bush II regime would not remedy their poor employment situation, but chose to believe otherwise? I single out this issue, as Tom Frank does, because in the 2000 election, in which Kansas showed its colour to be resolutely red, it was the economy, not the war, which was the central focus (one cannot say decisive, since it was the Supreme Court not the electorate that decided the actual outcome of the election). In all probability, the answer to this question is, no, Kansas's voters had no such knowledge.

It might seem appropriate, then, to revive the Marxist concept of 'false consciousness' to explain the turn to the right in the US. Without actually using this notion himself, Frank's account of the political metamorphosis of Kansas from a left-leaning, pro-worker, state to a right-wing and anti-worker state, in the space of only a few generations is clearly underpinned by the conviction that the people of Kansas 'know not what they do'. Not the least reason for his thinking this way is his view that this ideological shift flies in the face of the actual situation in Kansas which as economically depressed as it is would seem to be crying out for some old-fashioned worker solidarity. The point not to be missed here, as Žižek is fond of saying, is that they 'know not what they do' is *not* synonymous with 'I know very well, but all the same . . .'. Cynicism requires a degree of awareness of wrongdoing that quite simply is not present in the Kansas voters Frank interviews. On the contrary, they are as convinced of their rectitude as only the self-righteous can be – they have no doubt in their hearts that voting against the 'permissive' liberals is the right thing to do, regardless of the fact that the other party hasn't any chance and perhaps not even the intention of overturning the legislation protecting the right to abortion and the other hard-won civil rights they want withdrawn.

We must question, too, whether it is plausible to claim that the Kansas voters have disavowed the boundless amounts of contradictory knowledge constantly being put before them – e.g., the fact their vote supports a party that rewards with tax breaks the very people, namely 'decadent' Hollywood movie stars and mendacious CEOs, they find so risible. Is it possible that they have simply failed to process it? Are they unaware of what's going on, or fully aware but choosing to pretend otherwise? Is it cynicism or false consciousness that best describes their attitude? One cannot but share Frank's incredulity that Kansas's voters could be ignorant of the Republican Party's true agenda, namely to dismantle welfare programmes, cripple labour organizations, reduce taxes, and generally make things easier for big business profit-taking. Ultimately, Frank is so amazed at the lack of awareness of Kansas voters that he cannot help but laugh in a pitying Homer Simpson 'it is funny because it is true' like way at the saddening irony of it all. It is, however, the laughter of analytic despair. His tour of the state finds evidence virtually everywhere he looks that the right's agenda is anything but beneficial to the people of Kansas. Frank wears his colours and his heart on his sleeve, but one cannot dismiss as biased the social and economic devastation of Middle America he witnesses – boarded-up shop windows in small towns, collapsed property values, bankrupt family farms sold off to agribusiness conglomerates, job and capital flight, taxes being spent to provide sweetheart deals for multinational corporations, grievous environmental damage, and so on.

The cause of this devastation is open to debate only to the extent of determining whether it was the Left or the Right that authorized it. There can be no question that it is the handiwork of the latest phase of capitalism. Precisely because he wears his colours so openly, Frank is severest on the Left for the part they have had to play in either directly causing or just as culpably failing to halt the present slide into malaise of Middle America. Frank points an angry finger at former President Bill Clinton, whose centrist policies he holds directly responsible for the evisceration of the Left. In Frank's eyes, the Democrats have become, miserably enough, simply 'the other party that supports business'. In other words, the problem isn't that ultimately the Right is a worse choice than the Left, but they are both the 'worst choice' because both prioritize the market over all

other considerations. Neo-liberalism, as this market-oriented politics is usually labelled, although it is something of a misnomer since
it is neither new nor liberal in its outlook, is virtually the only choice,
regardless of which party happens to espouse it.

If a vote for either party is a vote for business, then that vote is
really an instance of what Žižek calls 'forced choice': in the US, and
most of the West today, you can vote Left or Right, but you cannot
vote against business. The exception to this rule might seem to be the
Green parties that have risen to prominence in most Western
nations, though not in the US, in the past two decades. But a vote
for the Greens isn't a vote against business or capital, it is a vote for
the consolation of an environmentally friendly business. In Britain
and elsewhere the traditional arch-rivals of environmentalism,
namely the Conservatives, have been able to adopt Green policies
without compromising their pro-business outlook because as many
businesses have discovered, environmental legislation can be good
for the bottom line: consumers will pay more for what they perceive
to be environmentally friendly products. But as many would also
argue, this is as much a sign of their desperation as anything else.
Blair so successfully made the centrist position his own and, more
importantly, so successfully positioned the centrist outlook as the
hegemonic worldview, the Conservatives have no other choice but to
try to win support by fighting the opposition on their own turf. As
every military theorist from Sun Tzu on says, there is no more
fraught strategy than this, because it leaves you with nowhere to turn
if your gambit fails.

Under such conditions, when there is no real choice, when neither
desire nor interest knows which way to turn, one can hardly chide
the electorate for choosing one party over the other. It is not as
though staunchly Left writers like Tom Frank think the Democrats
are actually better than the Republicans, or genuinely different from
the Republicans. Frank cleaves to an idea – or rather ideal – of the
Democrat Party embodied in the New Deal politics of the 1930s that
he himself shows has vanished from the political landscape. Frank's
conclusion that the Left has deserted its origins and turned itself
into a differently hued, but identical in all the essentials copy of the
Right, has to be read alongside his critique of the actual choices
voters make in Kansas today. It would be churlish indeed for the Left
to chastise the blue-collar voters of Kansas for not voting Democrat
when that party plainly has nothing to offer them in the way of

meaningful 'workerist' policy. Its doctrine is torn straight from the Republican Party playbook – business creates jobs, but it can't if it is unprofitable to do so, therefore to 'save' jobs, one has to govern in the interests of business, even when this means sacrificing such minimal worker protection as the minimum wage, unfair dismissal laws, occupational health and safety regulations, anti-discrimination and harassment laws, and so forth. If business demands the installation of Third World working conditions in the First World, to save it from 'having to' export jobs to the Third World, then so be it. Government has, by this logic, not only made itself hostage to business, and the rest of us with it, but has become its patsy too.

When business fails, it blames the government for strangling profitability with red tape, and then demands a bail-out package from the public purse. And government, mindful of the political fall-out job losses inevitably incur, tends to cave into this kind of extortion, setting in motion a cycle it cannot get out of except via a Leninist or Paulist gesture (actually it is an Adam Smith gesture – unprofitable businesses should be allowed to fail according to this doctrine Wall St espouses for others). Either government must let business go to the wall and accept the consequences, or it must assume full responsibility for the business by taking it over. Neither is a politically acceptable option today. So, if we are to do more than scoff at an electorate for failing to see that it isn't acting in its own best interest by continuing its rightward swerve, then we need to understand why this swerve appears to be the correct choice under the conditions in which it must be made.

Political commentators on the Left and Right are constantly torn between decrying the electorate as stupid for buying the slogans they are dished up and decrying the politicians for reducing complex issues to sound bites. We are told time and time again that this is the reality of politics today. If a political message doesn't sound good on the 6 o'clock news, it isn't going to get any airplay. If it can't be compressed into a headline, the major dailies won't run with it. If it doesn't hit a raw nerve, the shock jocks controlling talkback radio won't get behind it. Without these three things – reportage on the nightly news, constant headlines and talkback – you're politically dead. Of course, it cuts both ways. As John Kerry discovered in 2004, if you're at the wrong end of this, you can get blowtorched out of the race. But this just proves the rule. Kerry was never 'on message', as the communications professionals say. Although he was the Vietnam veteran and the other guy a draft-dodger who hid out in the National Service and never saw a shot fired in anger, it was Kerry that got done up in effigy and placed alongside Jane Fonda in the pantheon of traitors who stabbed 'real Americans' in the back.

Tom Frank argues that it was the abandoning of Labour that spelled the end of the Left. But I don't think this is the whole story. It doesn't explain how the Left and Right could come to their present state of imperceptibility. I would want to argue instead that it was the abandonment of the Welfare State, or what Jameson has more pointedly described as the political commitment to 'guaranteed life', that brought about its demise. If the Left is not committed to providing a decent standard of living for all people, then what does it stand for? Here the commitment to Labour that is an essential plank of Leftist parties actually gets in the way of the larger commitment to 'guaranteed life' because it puts the Left in the position of having to be, among other things, anti-immigration so as to defend wage levels from erosion due to the importation of cheap 'foreign' labour. In Australia, it was the Labor Party that inaugurated the 'White Australia' policy for precisely this reason. It mobilized xenophobia to create a protected labour market. Cynicism doesn't explain our situation because it doesn't provide a complicated enough account of how the electorate actually thinks and functions. Neither does false consciousness. What's needed is an analysis that shows how desire and interest can travel in different and indeed conflicting directions. Cynicism short-circuits the properly schizoanalytical contradiction the separation of desire and interest allows us to formulate and makes it seem as though it is possible to accommodate it. And that is precisely what schizoanalytical criticism should not allow: its purpose is exactly the opposite – to constantly point up the unendurability of the present.

Both the 'false consciousness' and 'cynicism' arguments are underpinned by what Deleuze calls a 'philosophical illusion' – both presume that there is a truth 'out there' somewhere which the good citizens of Kansas are either failing to see or seeing and failing to acknowledge. Marxist doctrine is conditioned by the utopian view that if awareness of the real conditions of existence becomes general enough then social change must occur because nobody could knowingly support capitalism as it really is. This is, in effect, the spectre Marx said was haunting Europe, the spectre of a truth that once known cannot be tolerated. 'False consciousness' and cynicism are conjured to explain the demoralizing fact that in spite of a century and more of consciousness-raising by the Left (in all its manifestations) after which no one could be left in any doubt as to the true nature of capitalist society, a spontaneous shift towards an equitable form of socialism has not only not occurred, but the minimal tokens of that utopia (such as the minimum wage, the public health system, old-age pension, and so on) are under threat of extinction. It is the schism between knowledge ('I know capitalism is an inequitable system') and action ('but all the same'), or lack thereof, as the case may be, that false consciousness and cynicism attempt to explain. They reason that if we knew the truth about our situation we would be compelled to act, therefore the fact that we do not act must mean we have disavowed the truth either by suppressing all knowledge of it from ourselves or by choosing not to acknowledge its implications. What we must prevent at all costs is cynicism becoming this new truth that is always already out there, because if that happens political thought, not to mention political action, is finished. The problem today is that while citizens as consumers can be motivated to complain or change brands, it is all but impossible to persuade them to act. Cynicism doesn't explain this state of affairs, it excuses it. In this sense, cynicism is the new name for what Foucault called fascism, as such *Anti-Oedipus'* message is as vital and urgent today as it was when it was first published.

CHAPTER 4

RECEPTION AND INFLUENCE

The reception of *Anti-Oedipus* has largely been decided by how well particular commentators have been able to cope with its infamously playful language. This is equally true of both the affirmative and the negative responses. Deleuze and Guattari enthusiasts can be just as muddled in their apprehension of *Anti-Oedipus* as the detractors. The difficulty of the rhetoric of *Anti-Oedipus* is such that it is an achievement in itself just to understand what they are trying to say. But this means figuring out what they are saying has taken priority over whether what they are saying is valid, cogent and indeed worth saying. There is in this respect little that has been written about Deleuze and Guattari that is genuinely critical, where that would mean evaluating their project from a position of understanding and determining its relative strengths and weaknesses. It is really only Deleuze and Guattari's detractors, those thinkers like Manfred Frank and Perry Anderson who regard schizoanalysis as wrong-headed, who tend to take this crucial step and inquire just what it is that Deleuze and Guattari have contributed to critical theory. But unfortunately, as I will briefly show, they do so from a position that is anything but adequate in its grasp of the complexities of their thought. On the other side of the coin, I hasten to add, the thinkers who have decided that Deleuze and Guattari's thought represents an advance on all other forms of thought tend not to see any need to defend their view, nor evaluate its premises. In the dozens of books that have been written about Deleuze and Guattari's work there are plenty of accounts of the superiority of their thought in relation to various other forms of thought, but too often these are straw figures projected out of Deleuze and Guattari's own work, such as the proverbial bogeyman the dialectic. This book will have achieved its purpose if by cutting through its heady rhetoric it has established the platform for a genuine critique of *Anti-Oedipus*.

The story of the reception of *Anti-Oedipus* needs to be stratified in two ways – firstly, there is an intergenerational split between Deleuze and Guattari's contemporaries and their students, the former tending to be cooler than the latter in their response; secondly, the response has varied from nation to nation, the furthest from France tending to be more enthusiastic than those closest to home.[1] Even today, there are more Deleuzians in Sydney than Paris. Deleuze and Guattari were undoubtedly a *cause célèbre* in France, particularly as *Anti-Oedipus* seemed to revive the spirit of May '68, but it was the intense international reception of their work that transformed them both into academic superstars. The number of books and articles on their work written in English far exceeds the number written in French (admittedly this number is artificially boosted by a new trend in the European academy, particularly in Scandinavian countries, to write in English regardless of the actual national language of origin). There is perhaps a third stratification that should be added here and that is the gap or rivalry between disciplines. As Fredric Jameson reminds us, what we know today as 'theory', an amorphous body of work that includes Deleuze and Guattari, first took root in Anglophone countries in French departments and not in the English, Philosophy or Cultural Studies departments where they are read today.[2] In the case of Australia, probably the most Deleuzified of any country, these three factors combined to produce a national explosion of Deleuzism: a brace of young scholars from the backblocks of Australia (among them, Rosi Braidotti, Anna Gibbs, Meaghan Morris, Stephen Muecke and Paul Patton) were drawn to France in the 1970s by the sense that something intellectually important was happening there, something more exciting than was available to them at home. After spending a year or more in Paris studying with Deleuze, Derrida, Foucault, Lyotard and others, these scholars returned home and radicalized the Australian academy, making it a veritable hotbed of theory.[3]

For a long time, the French reception of *Anti-Oedipus* was dominated by the jaundiced account given of it in Vincent Descombes *La Même et L'Autre*, first published in 1979 and translated a year later under the deceptive title of *Modern French Philosophy*. Descombes brands Deleuze and Guattari 'philosophers of desire' (a label that has stuck, mostly for the worse) and claims that *Anti-Oedipus* is primarily Nietzschean in inspiration. This (mis-)apprehension has been highly influential, particularly with Deleuze and Guattari's critics who tend to see this as reason enough to dismiss them without bothering to read *Anti-Oedipus* for themselves to see if Descombes' claim holds water. Using concepts drawn from Deleuze's book on Nietzsche published a decade before *Anti-Oedipus*, Descombes rewrites its argument in binary terms as an oscillation between reactive desire and active desire, failed revolutionaries or slaves on the one hand and authentic revolutionaries or masters on the other. He further claims that Deleuze and Guattari consign the concept of class struggle to the museum, thus evacuating Marx from their project altogether.[4] That this latter point is patently false I hope is clear. As we've already seen, *Anti-Oedipus* reinvigorates the concept of class struggle by linking it to desire and thus confronting the issue of how class solidarity comes about in the first place, or, as is more often the case fails to do so in spite of apparent need. If there is a binary in *Anti-Oedipus* it is between the concepts of desire and interest, which Deleuze and Guattari oppose in their account of the desire for oppression. The more damaging point, though, is the former one, which is in effect an accusation of idealism – and indeed, Descombes doesn't shy away from saying this directly.[5] Deleuze's Nietzschean affiliations are well known, and as I have shown, Nietzsche is important to *Anti-Oedipus*, but only insofar as his concepts further the materialist agenda of the project as a whole. I would suggest Nietzsche is deployed to intensify Marx, not negate him, and that it is always a revolutionary Marx who occupies centre stage in *Anti-Oedipus*. What *Anti-Oedipus* asks us to do, ultimately, is examine ourselves and understand our own inertia in the face of an egregious social system. It is Marx who demands we examine society in a systemic manner, and it is Nietzsche who demands that we recognize the degree to which society is a reflection of our desire.[6]

In France today the reception of *Anti-Oedipus* continues to be divided along the battle lines I mentioned above. Former students of Deleuze, like Éric Alliez, battle inconclusively with his former contemporaries, like Alain Badiou, one defending the purity of Deleuze and Guattari's thought, the other the purity of thought itself.[7] Badiou is largely dismissive of *Anti-Oedipus*, preferring to concentrate his attack on Deleuze's more overtly philosophical works.[8] This battle has its ugly side, as I've noted already, inasmuch that Guattari tends to be blamed for all the obscure passages in their collaborative works. He is held up by Badiou, in particular, as the great corruptor or contaminator of Deleuze, the one who turned him away from the pure path of philosophy. Ironically enough, if this has any truth in it, then it would mean Guattari deflected Deleuze away from the pursuit of a pure Niezschean line toward a more synthetic and overtly Marxian line. Slavoj Žižek uses this demonstrably false dichotomy between a good non-Guattarized Deleuze and a bad Guattarized Deleuze as the principal pivot of his book, *Organs without Bodies*, arguing that the former got himself into a philosophical hole that the latter failed to extricate him from. The dichotomy is false, as I've tried to show, because the theoretical backbone of *Anti-Oedipus* was constructed by Deleuze in his earlier books, particularly *Difference and Repetition*.[9] There is in effect a real continuity between the so-called good and bad Deleuze and not the split that Badiou and Žižek contend. Ultimately the 'two Deleuzes thesis' is like Deng Xiaoping's famous evaluation of Mao as 70 per cent good and 30 per cent bad, a way of selectively dealing with a powerful predecessor whose continuing influence is such that they cannot simply be dismissed. It enables Badiou and Žižek to accommodate themselves to that part of his philosophical legacy which conforms with their own take on things, particularly his re-readings of Nietzsche and Spinoza, while setting aside those aspects which would challenge their position without actually having to negate them in a theoretical sense. None of which should be taken to mean that interesting work on Deleuze and Guattari is not taking place in France right now, I hasten to add, only that (to the outsider at least) it seems to be oscillating in an oddly Oedipal fashion between the desire to save the father and the desire to kill him once and for all.

The German reception of *Anti-Oedipus*, much like the French reception, was for a similarly long time dominated by the work of a single author, namely philosopher and literary critic Manfred Frank, a student of the great hermeneuticist Hans Georg Gadamer.[10] Unfortunately, as with Descombes, Frank's influence was profoundly negative. His account of *Anti-Oedipus* had the effect of stifling at birth practically all interest in Deleuze and Guattari's work in Germany for well over a decade.[11] Its influence undoubtedly owes to the fact that unlike his contemporaries in the German academy, particularly Jürgen Habermas, Frank does not simply despatch Deleuze and Guattari with a single contemptuous line, but devotes four lengthy chapters to them in his tirade against all that has gone wrong in critical theory since the start of the 'French era' (as Jameson describes it), *What is Neostructuralism?*, which first appeared in German in 1984. His other targets are Jacques Lacan, Michel Foucault, Jacques Derrida and Jean-François Lyotard, all of whom he tars with the same brush as irrationalist thinkers who commit the folly of trying to conceive of an a-subjective philosophy, or a philosophy that isn't centred on a subject. Frank correctly interprets Deleuze and Guattari's work as building on the work of Foucault and Lacan, but rather than see this as a progressive development he sees it as evidence of a loss of reason. In his view Foucault and Lacan are already bad, that is already irrational, therefore building on their work is to take irrationality to new lengths. But for Frank the problem isn't simply that Deleuze and Guattari's work is philosophically incoherent, it goes deeper than that. The popularity of Deleuze and Guattari's work troubles him and in his view can only be lamented as the 'symptom of a crisis' which he describes as the spreading discontent, particularly in the younger generation, 'in the contemporary condition of our souls and our culture'.[12] He thus makes their work emblematic for all that is wrong with critical theory today and in this way fails to do the very thing he urges his readers to do, which is 'to seriously accept' the 'challenge' of their thought.[13]

Frank clearly finds *Anti-Oedipus* heavy going. At one point he admits that its rhetoric is inaccessible to him and at another that he isn't sure why a particular term (molecular) is used.[14] Consequently we aren't surprised when he fails to perceive the distinction between pathological and non-pathological instances of desiring-production. He thus accuses Deleuze and Guattari of 'neovitalism' for infusing machines with life, but as we have seen, this is not at all Deleuze and Guattari's position.[15] It is only the schizophrenic in the full flight of their illness that perceives the world this way and what's more it is a sign of the presence of the illness that they see the world this way. In spite of his numerous misreadings of *Anti-Oedipus* – which I won't list precisely because they are so numerous – Frank nevertheless raises a crucial question, one that has troubled most if not all politically conscious readers of Deleuze and Guattari: in whose name do the authors fight?[16] Perry Anderson's fear that Deleuze and Guattari have pulverized the subject is emblematic of a deep concern amongst the more strategically oriented critics that in fact Deleuze and Guattari speak for no one and nothing. The most extreme version of this was the initial feminist response, led by Luce Irigaray and reinforced by Alice Jardine, that having dismembered the body, Deleuze and Guattari had destroyed the very source of a feminist politics, namely corporeally situated sexual difference.[17] A body construed only as a loose coalition of disconnected, libidinal- ized parts is, feminist scholars feared, unable to give rise to a feminist politics, and in that sense can only be construed as a continuation of patriarchal theory as usual. Marxist scholars like Alex Callinicos latched onto Deleuze's Nietzschean past and interpreted *Anti- Oedipus* as an exercise in perspectivism, or what amounts to the same thing (for Callinicos at any rate), extreme relativism.[18] But this is neither a good interpretation of Deleuze and Guattari nor a good interpretation of Nietzsche. If, as Jameson has argued, Hegel is a codeword in French critical theory for Stalin, then one wonders what Nietzsche is a codeword for in Anglo-American critical theory because there is no greater insult in its lexicon than the label 'Nietzschean'.[19] If Callinicos' usage is anything to go by, I suspect it stands for 'primitivist', which in the Marxist logic of stages (in which the primitive necessarily precedes capital), actually amounts to saying someone is 'proto-capitalist'. This would be consistent with Žižek's reading of Deleuze and Guattari as the ideologists of late capitalism.

As is so often the case with charismatic figures, as testimony from former students and colleagues assure us Deleuze and Guattari were, one needs to get away from them in order to think clearly, which perhaps explains why it was the students from abroad – Rosi Braidotti, Michael Hardt, Eugene Holland, Brian Massumi, Paul Patton and others – who have proven to be the most significant exponents of their work. But with the signal exception of Holland, who has written an introduction to *Anti-Oedipus*, this generation of Deleuze scholars has tended to favour *A Thousand Plateaus* rather than *Anti-Oedipus*. Indicatively, Massumi's *User's Guide to Capitalism and Schizophrenia* gives scant attention to *Anti-Oedipus* and for the most part assumes that *A Thousand Plateaus* is a reca- pitulation and dare I say a sublation of its prequel. The second gen- eration of Deleuze scholars – the scholars who followed the path blazed by Braidotti, Hardt, Holland, Massumi and Patton – such as myself, but also Claire Colebrook, Manuel DeLanda, Gregg Lambert, as well as many others, have tended to do the same thing (I am speaking very generally). The point I want to make here, in conclusion, is that insofar as we conflate *Anti-Oedipus* with *A Thousand Plateaus*, we obscure the fact that *Anti-Oedipus* is a revolutionary book, whereas *A Thousand Plateaus* is not. In 1972 Deleuze and Guattari wanted to change society, almost at any cost; but by 1980, when the second volume appeared, they had pulled back from their previous radical stance, and where before they'd said change by any means necessary, now they asked for restraint. Near to the end of his life, in *L'Abécédaire*, Deleuze explained that he'd seen too many of his students die and felt that he somehow had to caution them against extreme action. But the radical project of *Anti-Oedipus* should not be allowed to disappear this way into the miasma of regret for the shattered lives and broken dreams of a handful of individuals. Its project was and remains to change society as a whole by questioning why *we* have allowed and indeed actively desired it to be the way it is. The truth it proclaims is that we have the society we deserve and that if we would have things otherwise then it is up to us to use our desire to make things different from how they are. *Anti-Oedipus* is a Utopian book in the strictest sense: it offers a blueprint for a different world, not by describing that world in fantastic terms, but by showing the way out of this one. And that remains a worthwhile but incomplete project.[20]

NOTES

1. DELEUZE AND GUATTARI IN CONTEXT

1 Anderson 1983: 39.
2 Anderson 1983: 51.
3 Anderson 1983: 27.
4 Jameson 1990: 4.
5 Badiou 2005: 136.
6 Reported in the International News section of *The Guardian*, 5 May 2007, p. 21.
7 Nadaud 2006: 12.
8 Negri 2004: 46.
9 For an excellent discussion of this apparent contradiction in Deleuze's approach to 'praxis' see Thoburn 2003: 35–7.
10 He was involved in GIP for instance and later spoke out against the treatment of Palestinians, as well as the first Gulf War.
11 It is now available on DVD.
12 Of those students, Deleuze said: 'I never told that audience what they meant to me, what they gave me. [. . .] It was like an echo chamber, a feedback loop, in which an idea reappeared after going, as it were, through various filters. It was there I realised how much philosophy needs not only a philosophical understanding, through concepts, but a nonphilosophical understanding, rooted in percepts and affects. You need both.' (D, 139/191).
13 Pinhas also used Deleuze's voice in other ways, combining it with music to produce Deleuze-inspired electronica of a peculiarly haunting variety.
14 Interestingly enough, Guattari described himself as being heavily influenced by Sartre, even going so far as to admit certain concepts like deterritorialization are simply Sartre's in disguise.
15 Tournier 1988: 128.
16 Negri 2004: 46. As Negri records here, it was Guattari who arranged for Negri's relocation from Italy to France in the early 1980s with the help of Amnesty International. They collaborated on a variety of political projects, including an ultimately forlorn but important attempt to forge

an alliance between the Reds and the Greens, and produced a manifesto, *Communists Like Us: New Spaces of Liberty, New Lines of Alliance* (1985), which foreshadows many of themes Negri would take up in his collaborative work with Michael Hardt, especially *Empire* (2000).

17 For a detailed analysis of this publication see Genosko 2007. The full text of the journal can now be viewed on the web at: www.criticalsecret.com/n8/quer/4per/pedo/01.htm.

18 For a more detailed account of Oury's work, see the important interview: 'The Hospital is Ill' (Oury 2007).

19 Reflecting on the meeting with Lacan to discuss *Anti-Oedipus*, Guattari wrote in his diary that he felt something had broken between them (AOP, 344/not included in French edition).

20 Nadaud 2006.

21 Genosko 2002: 16.

22 'May '68 was the largest mass movement in French history, the biggest strike in the history of the French workers' movement [involving some 9 million workers], and the only "general" insurrection the overdeveloped world has known since World War II. It was the first general strike that extended beyond the traditional centres of industrial production to include workers in the service industries, the communication and culture industries – the whole sphere of social reproduction. No professional sector, no category of worker was unaffected by the strike; no region, city, or village in France was untouched.' (Ross 2002: 4).

23 Ross 2002: 6.

24 'May '68 came as a shock to Gilles and me, as to many others: we didn't know each other, but this book, now, is nevertheless a result of May.' (N, 15/26).

25 Ross 2002: 106; 116.

26 For a more contemporary example one might think of the anti-World Trade Organisation protest in Seattle in November 1999, which (though not on the scale of May '68) famously united blue collar workers and environmentalists in protest against what they rightly saw as the instauration of a new world order determined to make the whole planet congenial to the business interests of the major powers. See Buchanan and Parr 2006: 11–14.

27 Similarly they rejected as pointless the shrill demand for self-criticism the Maoists made, arguing that it did nothing to engage power as it actually functions. As Deleuze put it, 'in May 1968 the leftists lost a lot of time insisting that professors engage in public self-criticism as agents of bourgeois ideology. It's stupid, and it simply fuels the masochistic impulses of academics.' (CY, 56).

28 They certainly didn't share the view of commentators like Raymond Aron and (much more recently) Pierre Nora who declared that nothing happened that May. Nor would they go along with the New Philosophers' attempt a decade later to bury the memory of May '68 altogether. See Ross 2002: 67; 171.

29 Thus, I have to disagree with Peter Hallward (2006: 7) when he argues rather that Deleuze's work has little to offer politically speaking because

Deleuze fails to live up to Marx's dictum that philosophy should not simply try to understand society, it should try to change it as well. In my view, he caricatures Deleuze as a contemplative philosopher whose thought somehow resists doing what needs to be done. For Deleuze, theoretical work is in itself a political act because it creates new conditions for thought and there is no more potent formula for change than the changing of ideas and attitudes. In this regard, Deleuze's political thought is compatible with the positions outlined by Holloway (2005) and George (2004).

30 As Ronald Bogue (1989: 6) observes the renown of *Anti-Oedipus* was something of a double-edged sword. Deleuze and Guattari 'became symbols of anti-psychiatry and the spirit of May, and as a result the broader concerns that informed *Anti-Oedipus* were often ignored'.

31 Jameson 1990: 5.

32 Ross 2002: 95.

33 Ross 2002: 95.

34 The reference is to Robert Musil's *Der Mann ohne Eigenschaften* (*The Man Without Qualities*) which, as Deleuze notes, recalls Pierre and Isabel in Herman Melville's *Pierre, or the Ambiguities* (CC, 74). For a more detailed consideration the incestuous pair in Musil and Melville from a Deleuzian perspective, see Buchanan 2000: 93–116.

35 Ross 2002: 26.

36 Ross 2002:38.

37 Fields 1984: 149.

38 Dine 1994: 220.

39 Fields 1984: 151.

40 Ross 2002: 80.

41 Ross 2002: 91.

42 Elsewhere, I argue that this is the essential lesson to be drawn from the US invasion of Iraq in 2003 (Buchanan 2006c: 25).

43 Ross 2002: 91. On a practical level, too, it was the anti-Vietnam groups, like the CVN and CVB, both of which formed in 1967, which provided the organizational nuclei that helped escalate May '68 from a localized student protest to nationwide strike.

44 As Nicholas Thoburn (2003) has demonstrated, the workers' movements in Italy were very important to Deleuze and Guattari.

45 Ross 2002: 130.

46 Jameson 1994.

47 Ross 2002: 170.

2. OVERVIEW OF THEMES

1 Baudrillard 1987: 39.

2 See Hardt 1993: 104–7.

3 A different translation of this piece can also be found in Foucault (1977).

4 It is worth noting here that Foucault's book on prisons, *Discipline and Punish*, had not yet appeared. Moreover, when it was finally published

three years after *Anti-Oedipus* it carried a footnote expressing a significant debt to the work of Deleuze and Guattari. See Foucault 1975: 309n2.
5 Cockburn 2006: 82–99.
6 Klein 2000: 281.
7 Klein 2000: 76.
8 Frank 1997: 185–204.
9 This is perhaps the moment to say something in reply to Slavoj Žižek's (2004: 183–192) provocative suggestion that Deleuze is the ideologist of late capitalism. He offers two points in justification of this claim: firstly, citing Jean-Jacques Lecercle's amusing anecdote of witnessing a yuppie reading Deleuze and Guattari on a train and imagining their bewilderment, Žižek asks us to contemplate the opposite scenario of a yuppie reading Deleuze and Guattari on a train and recognizing in it several existential imperatives already familiar to him. If one were to accept this reasoning, that Deleuze and Guattari are ideologists of late capitalism by virtue of the fact that some of their readers happen to find confirmation of their capitalist worldview in their work, then we'd have to jettison practically every thinker and writer on the Left because nobody has taken the Left's emphasis on labour, value and capital, more seriously than the Right. Indeed, it is precisely the neo-liberals who most fully embrace Althusser's famous doctrinal claim that the ultimate determining instance is the economic. Was this not what Margaret Thatcher meant by her infamous slogan 'There is no alternative'? Secondly, he claims that the book *Netocracy*, written by two Swedish writers Alexander Bard and Jan Soderqvist, is inspired by Deleuze and Guattari and that means that Deleuze and Guattari are ideologists of late capitalism. Even if we accept the rather dubious claim that this book which only cites Deleuze and Guattari a handful of times is inspired by their work, that is not by itself sufficient to justify the conclusion that Deleuze and Guattari would endorse its contents. Žižek's second exhibit is thus fashioned in the same way as the first, and though it scarcely seems possible it is even less convincing. If one were to accept this line of argument one would have to set aside the very idea of criticism itself. It would mean in effect that every text written in the name of, or inspired by a master thinker like Deleuze, but also Žižek as well, is an irreducible judgement on that thinker. If that were the case then every bad article I read claiming to be inspired by Žižek's work has to be read as a judgement on him too. That he is unwilling to accept this position (as I am) is blatantly apparent in his many rejoinders to Judith Butler, Michael Hardt and Toni Negri, and especially Ernesto Laclau.
10 For an exhaustive account of the influences on and sources of Deleuze and Guattari's conception of the unconscious, albeit one that takes the strange decision to give relatively little attention to *Anti-Oedipus*, see Kerslake (2007).
11 Freud 1991: 199.
12 Lacan's essay 'The Freudian Thing', included in *Écrits*, provides an important gloss of the problems involved in this particular translation. See Lacan 2006: 347.

13 See the 'Editor's Introduction' to Freud's essay 'The Ego and the Id' in Freud 1991: 345.
14 Todd May (2005: 121) takes precisely this line in his discussion of Deleuze and Guattari's concept of machines.
15 Freud 1991: 397.
16 See Freud 1991: 206–7.
17 Freud 1976: 364.
18 I examine this issue from a different angle in Buchanan 2000: 175–6.
19 Freud 1979: 186–9.
20 This is why Bettelheim remains important to Deleuze and Guattari in spite of his obvious bias toward an Oedipal or pre-Oedipal interpretation of the cause of schizophrenia, and the blame he heaps upon parents as a result. Bettelheim (1967: 316) reinterprets the Oedipal myth as a warning to parents that if they don't stay in touch with their children, if they blind their children to the truth of existence, then they will wind up like Oedipus. In spite of his Freudian predilection, Bettelheim is nonetheless willing to admit to the idea that schizophrenia is an autonomous productive force in its own right, which in full flight owes little to the actions of the parents (AO, 40/45).
21 See Freud 1979.

3. READING THE TEXT

1 See Anderson 1983: 55.
2 Laing 1990: 41.
3 Büchner 1993: 142.
4 As an aside, we may note that this impression of schizophrenia is of a piece with Fredric Jameson's conception of modernism (as the essential precursor to postmodernism) as it is summed up in the marvellous quote from Rimbaud concerning the magical flowers 'that look back at you' (Jameson 1991: 10). It is probably worth adding, on this score, that Jameson's conception of schizophrenia, which he associates with post-modernity, is derived from Lacan not Deleuze and Guattari. See Buchanan 2000: 159–64.
5 Žižek 1991: 109–11.
6 Hardt and Negri 2000: 214–18.
7 A preliminary working out of the essential components of the three syntheses of time are to be found in Deleuze's earlier books, particularly *Bergonism* (chapters 3 and 4) and *Proust and Signs* (chapter 5). *Cinema 1* and *Cinema 2* are the extension of these syntheses to their logical limits.
8 Symptomatically, there is no entry for passive synthesis in either *Gilles Deleuze: Key Concepts*, edited by Charles Stivale, or in the glossary appended to Mark Bonta and John Protevi's *Deleuze and Geophilosophy: A Guide and Glossary*. But see Keith Faulkner's, *Deleuze and the Three Syntheses of Time*, Jay Lampert's *Deleuze and the Philosophy of History*, and James Williams' account of the three syntheses of time in *Gilles Deleuze's Difference and Repetition*.

9 Hallward 2006: 162.
10 This is a complex issue, and not one I can do justice to here. I deal with this problematic more fully in Buchanan 2000: 73–89.
11 As will become clear in what follows, Brian Massumi's (1992: 56) definitions of both active and passive synthesis as 'evaluations' is inaccurate. They are not as he says 'approximate terms', but real and distinct processes locked in mutual presupposition. Massumi correctly identifies that something – his example is the wind – may be passive in one context and active in another, but overlooks the more important fact that everything is first of all passive in relation to itself, and then active in relation to the external world.
12 Arrighi 1994: 5.
13 This is why in recent decades throughout most of the developed world, capital has either pulled out of manufacturing altogether and embraced what some people call the 'knowledge' or 'information' economy, or relocated its operations to the Third World, thus relieving itself of the impediment to profitability presented by the relatively inflexible labour and regulatory environment of the First World.
14 Arrighi 1994: 6.
15 This is why Deleuze and Guattari argue that the limits of capital are immanent: capital constantly pushes up against its limits, and may from time to time enter into periods of crisis, but somehow it always manages to reset its limits and persevere.
16 Marx 1976: 874–5.
17 Marx 1976: 875.
18 Marx 1976: 875.
19 Marx 1976: 451.
20 Marx 1976: 451.
21 Althusser 1971: 133.
22 Althusser 1971:171–2.
23 Davis 2006: 185.
24 Davis 2006: 80.
25 As Žižek points out, God's gift of freedom to humanity is an example par excellence of the paradox of the 'forced choice': 'Man is given freedom – with the expectation that he will not (mis)use it to break free from the Creator, that is, to become really free.' (Žižek 2006: 96).
26 Althusser 1971: 219.
27 To which they add: 'As if every great doctrine were not a *combined formation*, constructed from bits and pieces, various intermingled codes and flux, partial elements and derivatives, that constitute its very life or its becoming. As if we could reproach someone for having an ambiguous relationship with psychoanalysis, without first mentioning that psychoanalysis owes its existence to a relationship, theoretically and practically ambiguous, with what it discovers and the forces that it wields.' (AO, 128/140).
28 'Retention is the primary function of the family: it is a matter of learning what elements of desiring-production the family is going to reject, what it is going to retain, what it is going to direct along the dead-end

roads leading to its own undifferentiated (the miasma), and what on the contrary it is going to lead down the paths of a contagious and reproducible differentiation. For the family creates at the same time its disgraces and its honours, the nondifferentiation of its neurosis and the differentiation of its ideal, which are distinguishable only in appearance.' (AO, 136/148).

29 We will consider practical implications of the legitimate and illegitimate uses of the three syntheses in more detail in the next section.

30 Badiou 2000: 11–12. I should add that Deleuze and Guattari themselves describe the phallus as being like 'the One in negative theology' (AO, 67/70).

31 Ironically, if one were to grant that such a thing as 'penis envy' existed, then it would be men not women who suffer from it the most severely, because while men 'have' a penis already and women do not, it is never adequate in their eyes, never adequate to protect them from the necessity of having to assume a passive attitude towards other men. The castrating effect of the phallus is in this sense doubled: men not only fear its loss, but also have the feeling that it is already lost (that it is a useless 'surplus').

32 Although they don't discuss methods for doing this here, they do insist that 'in place of the benevolent pseudo neutrality of the Oedipal analyst, who wants and understands only daddy and mommy, we must substitute a malevolent, an openly malevolent activity: your Oedipus is a fucking drag, keep it up and the analysis will be stopped, or else we'll apply a shock treatment to you!' (AO, 123/134).

33 I discuss this example at greater length in Buchanan 2006d: 60–3.

34 Jameson 1992: 26.

35 Žižek 2001: 134.

36 I am referring here to Žižek's (1991: 104) experiment of imagining Hitchcock's *The Birds* without any birds.

37 In this way, '*we pass from detachable partial objects to the detached complete object, from which global persons derive by an assigning of lack*' (AO, 81/87).

38 Acting together or for the sake of individual survival is not collective action and should not be mistaken for action undertaken for the sake of the common good. In terms of Alain Badiou's ethics, this type of survivalist collective action corresponds to the evil of 'simulacra' or what he also calls 'terror' because it mimics genuine common good collective action, and speaks in the name of the common cause, but its intentions are otherwise. Under the guise of a desire for common cause, what is in fact realized is the desire for a common enemy. Badiou 2001: 72–7.

39 Interestingly enough, Deleuze does not draw this conclusion himself in his books on cinema, despite the fact that his mapping of the narrative logic of prewar cinema, particularly film noir, is motivated by lack. The notions of the small and large form, SAS' and ASA', are both motivated by lack – in the first example, something is lacking in the situation which demands an action to rectify it, and in the second something is lacking

in an action and this gives rise to an unsatisfactory situation demanding a changed action. See C1, 182–8/243–50.

40 On a related point, it also explains Deleuze's famous distaste for the question and answer mode of interviews and his insistence on the need for philosophers to be allowed to pose their own questions.

41 Jameson 1981: 58.

42 As readers of *What is Philosophy?* will be aware, Deleuze and Guattari's final project was devoted to overcoming what they both saw as the tyranny of opinion.

43 Jameson 1981: 59.

44 Jameson 1981: 217.

45 Jameson 1981: 117.

46 Jameson 1981: 114.

47 Jameson 1981: 201.

48 Badiou (2005: 136) suggests that such moments in history might usefully be termed 'Thermidorean'.

49 Conrad 2000: 304.

50 Conrad 2000: 209.

51 Conrad 2000: 100.

52 DeLanda 2006: 10–19.

53 The importance of this omission will become clearer in the next section when I discuss the capture of desire.

54 This will perhaps surprise those readers of Deleuze and Guattari who see this concept as a site of experimentation or freedom. But these two perspectives are not mutually incompatible – selection, which is the supreme function of the body without organs, must by definition mean actively choosing between an array of options, with some being taken and others passed over. It is this capacity for repression that Deleuze and Guattari seize upon in their explanation of the formation of social machines.

55 Indeed, as readers of *A Thousand Plateaus* would be aware, one could not begin to understand the concept of becoming without them. By the same token, what is the rhizome if it is not a valorization of alliance over affiliation?

56 This structure is preserved in contemporary Western mythologizations of love, particularly in popular music, wherein we give our love to the person who stole our heart.

57 Marx 1976: 103. For an extended discussion of this point see Buchanan 2000: 17–19.

58 Marx 1973: 102. Deleuze and Guattari cite this passage themselves (AO, 240–1/261), but the English translation does not agree with the English source the translators cite, i.e., the source I have cited, so for that reason I have gone directly to the source.

59 Jameson 1988b: 25. For a useful discussion and extension of Jameson's concept, see Žižek 2002: 182–8.

60 Naomi Klein describes this situation as 'one-way strip poker' whereby 'the United States and Europe – via the World Bank, the International Monetary Fund and the World Trade Organisation – tell the developing

world, "You take down your trade barriers and we'll keep ours up"'.
(Klein 2007: 10).

61 'Debt repayments today represent a substantial net transfer of wealth
from the working poor of the Third World to the coffers of international
finance capital.' Parenti 1995: 21.

62 For instance, the housing booms that have (periodically) gripped most of
the First World nations in the past two decades are compelling proof of
the accuracy of this insight. By lowering interest rates and thereby
increasing the affordability of borrowing, banks have fuelled a desire for
housing at once expansionist and proprietorial that has paradoxically
reduced the affordability of housing itself by pushing up prices at expo-
nential rate. Mortgages dominate the national agendas of First World
countries and no issue – not even an illegal, unjust war – is more important to their electorates than the need to maintain low interest rates at a
steady state. Despite the very real personal gains made by some housing
investors, and the equally real penalties those excluded from the market
must endure, the housing boom has not and cannot close the gap between
the two types of money. For more on this topic from a Deleuzian point
of view, see Buchanan 2006d: 144–8.

63 Parenti 1995: 6–14.

64 'Marx's once scandalous thesis that governments are simple business
agents for international capital is today an obvious fact on which "liberals" and "socialists" agree. The absolute identification of politics with
the management of capital is no longer the shameful secret hidden
behind the "forms" of democracy; it is the openly declared truth by
which our governments acquire legitimacy.' (Rancière 1999: 113). Or, as
Deleuze and Guattari themselves put it: 'Never before has a State lost so
much of its power in order to enter with so much force into the service
of the signs of economic power.' (AO, 274/300).

65 The 'axiomatic is not the invention of capitalism, since it is identical with
capital itself. On the contrary, capitalism is its offspring, its result.
Capitalism merely ensures the regulation of the axiomatic . . .' (AO,
274/300).

66 Rancière 1999: 110.

67 'Sadly, psychologists have shown that, whereas depression is prominent
among first-generation immigrants who experience adaptational
difficulties, schizophrenia predominates among maladjusted second-
generation migrants. Such youth turn to Islamism in order to resolve
what is often a severe and protracted identity crisis.' (Wolin, 2007:
26).

68 This is of course the basic thrust of Hardt and Negri's (2000) 'multitude'
thesis: according to their view of things, capitalism is bringing about
changes in the very composition of society that have already put in
motion developments that will ultimately result in the supersession of
capitalism by a new system.

69 Brink 2000: 306.

70 Cf. Fitrakis, Rosenfeld and Wasserman 2006.

NOTES

71 For instance, see Žižek 2001: 109. It must be mentioned, too, that Žižek draws very heavily on Peter Sloterdijk's *Critique of Cynical Reason.*
72 Žižek 2004a: 95.

4. RECEPTION AND INFLUENCE

1 For reasons of space. I will consider only the Australian, American, French and German responses to Deleuze and Guattari's work. From even this limited survey, however, it is obvious that a more global comparative analysis of the national receptions of their work would be rewarding.
2 Jameson 2006: 121–4. That this was true of the reception of Deleuze and Guattari in the US can be seen in the fact that his first commentators there were all from French or Comparative Literature programmes, e.g., Ronald Bogue, Michael Hardt, Eugene Holland, Fredric Jameson, Alice Jardine, Brian Massumi and Charles Stivale.
3 This in turn promoted the growth of Cultural Studies by setting aside the intuitionism that dominated literary studies until then (a hangover from the Richards and Leavis era), and by politicizing the unquestioned assumptions of Anthropology and History departments schooled in the ways of empire, and ultimately by collapsing the boundaries between text and context. Although Cultural Studies in Australia today tends to be rather reserved about theory, it would never have developed the way it has if theory had not blossomed there first.
4 Descombes 1980: 178.
5 Descombes 1980: 178.
6 Eugene Holland (1999: 11–13) offers a slightly different, though not contradictory, account of the significance of Nietzsche to Deleuze and Guattari. He positions Nietzsche as a kind of 'vanishing mediator' bridging Freud and Marx. I do not think this is necessarily a wrong way of looking at things, but in my view it overemphasizes the structural importance of Nietzsche. In Holland's account, the basic architecture of *Anti-Oedipus* is taken from Nietzsche, whereas I have suggested Nietzsche functions more as a 'tensor' or 'intensifier' of a blueprint derived from Marx.
7 Cf. Alliez 2006 and Badiou 2000. But see also David-Ménard 2005: 115–27.
8 Badiou 2000. Sadly, while Deleuzians have been quick to reject Žižek's reading of Deleuze, they have been much less vocal in their response to Badiou, even though it is a much more egregious misreading of Deleuze than Žižek (not the least because it is a much more attentive reading).
9 It is almost impossible to say enough bad things about Žižek's book, but as it has already been repudiated at length by several other scholars, there is no need for me to rehearse in detail here all the reasons why it is a bad book – see, for example, Berressem (2005), Lambert (2006: 81–101) and Smith (2004). It is, however, worth adding a brief comment about Žižek's reply to criticism of this book because it is bizarre even by

his standards. In separate replies to Smith (Žižek 2004b) and myself (Žižek 2005), he claims that critics have ignored the fact that his book is making a serious proposition, namely that Deleuze and Guattari's concept of the unconscious is in fact Jungian in conception. What is bizarre about this response is that one would look in vain in *Organs without Bodies* to find this claim actually being made. It seems that in addition to the charge of not reading Deleuze and Guattari very well we have to add the charge that Žižek doesn't read Žižek very well. His evidence for this supposed Jungian connection is flimsy indeed: apparently Jung used the word 'rhizome' in a memoir written in 1961. Does this make Deleuze and Guattari Jungian? Hardly. Similarly, the fact that Deleuze used Jung in his critique of Freud in his book on Masoch no more makes him Jungian than the fact that Žižek sometimes uses Deleuze in a positive fashion makes him Deleuzian. The more serious claim is that Deleuze and Guattari's concept of the unconscious is ultimately 'primitive', meaning pre-social. This claim is patently false and can be repudiated very simply by remembering that Deleuze and Guattari's most fundamental point in *Anti-Oedipus* is that unconscious desire is part of the very infrastructure of society and vice versa.

10 For a more detailed explanation of why the German reception of Deleuze and Guattari's work was so unenthusiastic to begin with, see Balke (1996). Balke does not lay blame at Frank's door as I have, but his description of the reasons why German scholars were initially so cool towards Deleuze and Guattari is essentially a portrait of Frank's take on their work.

11 The one major exception to this rule is Klaus Theweleit, whose magnificent two-volume history of the Brownshirts, *Männerphantasien* (1977), translated as *Male Fantasies* (1987), makes extensive use of *Anti-Oedipus*. If it is not, finally, a Deleuzian book, that is because it translates Deleuze and Guattari's concept of the machine back into fantasy, making it once again the content of dreams rather than the source.

12 Frank 1989: 317.

13 Frank 1989: 318.

14 Frank 1989: 329; 333.

15 Frank 1989: 319.

16 Frank 1989: 341.

17 Cf. Irigaray 1985: 106–18; Jardine 1985: 208–23. But see Colebrook 2000.

18 Cf. Callinicos 1982: 85–111; 1989: 83–91. See also Dews 1987: 131–43.

19 From this perspective, defending Deleuze and Guattari's Niezschean inspiration, as Paul Patton (1988) does, is of ambiguous value: it concedes too much ground to the opposition because it allows them to set the terms of the debate. On this issue, I prefer Deleuze and Guattari's own template, and reject both the problem and the solution and come at it from a different angle altogether, namely the perspective of Utopia.

20 Thus Lotringer's (2001: 155) abusive idea that Deleuze and Guattari left behind no model to be followed, nor a theory to be applied, and actively discouraged anyone from learning from their thought, has simply to be

rejected as nonsense. They very clearly wanted to change society, that they left behind no blueprint or programme of change is beside the point. What they realized is that change could only come about if we – meaning society as a whole – could be made to give up our addiction to the present regime. Such a project is properly called 'Utopian'. That Lotringer thinks Deleuze and Guattari hated such a notion shows how very poorly he has read them – one has only to see how approvingly they cite Fourier in *Anti-Oedipus*, to give only one example, to see how important Utopia is to their work.

FURTHER READING

Deleuze and Guattari were eclectic in their approach to writing *Anti-Oedipus*, a fact that is evident on virtually every page. They bring to bear an incredible range of source material from literally all disciplines, from anthropology and comparative religion to philosophy, psychoanalysis and the hard sciences. This can be quite bewildering. The constant question raised by new readers of Deleuze and Guattari's work is whether or not there is anything to be gained by either reading some of Deleuze's previous books (*Anti-Oedipus* was Guattari's first published book), or their original sources. My answer to both these questions is a cautious 'yes', but with two qualifications: first, Deleuze's previous books should be read with an eye toward the real continuity in his work from his first to his last books, thereby avoiding the casuistry of the 'two Deleuzes' thesis; second, one has to recognize that Deleuze and Guattari were 'selective' readers to use Michael Hardt's important methodological stipulation (Hardt 1993: xix). They use other thinkers to advance their own project and at no time do they try to give a systematic account of any of the works they draw on – not Freud, not Marx, not Lacan, not anyone. As such it is futile to ask whether they are really Nietzschean or Lacanian, or indeed whether they got their Nietzsche or Lacan right. This isn't to let them off the hook by any means, but it is to say that they should be read in terms of the cogency of their creation. The sole question of relevance is whether or not schizoanalysis works. In order to be able to make that judgement it is, to be sure, helpful to have an idea of where they are coming from. The following suggestions for further reading are offered then as a preliminary guide for how to get started reading Deleuze and Guattari.

Works by Deleuze

I am not convinced that extensive pre-reading of Deleuze's previous books is all that helpful in understanding *Anti-Oedipus*. In some respects, it could even be said that it is redundant inasmuch that, as I've argued here, *Anti-Oedipus* picks up on ideas Deleuze developed in earlier work and expands on them, giving them a more practical edge. For exactly the same reason, though, it could be said that interrogating his previous work is vital. That said, I would recommend the following selections from Deleuze's work: chapter 2 of *Difference and Repetition*, which details Deleuze's theory of passive synthesis; chapter 13 of *The Logic of Sense*, which is an account of Artaud's notion of the body without organs; chapter 5 of *Empiricism and Subjectivity*, which gives an account of the notion that relations are external to their terms; and lastly chapter 3 of *Nietzsche and Philosophy* on critique.

As would be obvious from this book, Deleuze and Guattari's interviews, given and published in the years after *Anti-Oedipus* appeared, are also extremely helpful. So one should certainly also look at *Dialogues* and *Negotiations*.

Works by Guattari

Guattari's recently published diary and working notes, *The Anti-Oedipus Papers*, is an invaluable resource for anyone interested in understanding *Anti-Oedipus*. Particularly useful, in my opinion, is the diary, because here one sees Guattari applying his ideas and concepts to himself. It offers an extremely interesting example of schizoanalysis as a form of self-analysis.

Works by other authors

I have broken this list into three broad categories of sources: (1) psychoanalysis; (2) historical materialism; and (3) literature. The lists are in descending order of importance. I have only included those works which are readily available in English.

Psychoanalysis
Freud: Deleuze and Guattari refer explicitly and extensively to several works by Freud, making it practically impossible for any reader ignorant of these texts to make sense of their arguments. In particular,

one must at least read the essay on Schreber, 'Psychoanalytic Notes on an Autobiographical Account of a Case of Paranoia' (in volume 12 of the *Standard Edition* [SE] of Freud's work). One might also read in conjunction with this Schreber's *Memoirs of My Nervous Illness*. Also useful are the following essays by Freud: 'A Child is Being Beaten' (SE, vol 17), 'Analysis Terminable and Interminable' (SE, vol 23), 'The Unconscious' (SE, vol 14), and 'The Ego and the Id' (SE, vol 19). This list could be expanded quite easily, but this is sufficient as a starting point.

Lacan: Deleuze and Guattari (particularly Guattari who was a fully trained member of Lacan's school), were clearly familiar with most if not all Lacan's work. Achieving this sort of familiarity is a life's work in itself. My recommendation is that one should read at least a couple of Lacan's essays as well as one good introduction to his work such as Elizabeth Grosz's *Jacques Lacan: A Feminist Introduction* or Slavoj Žižek's *Looking Awry*. The key Lacan essays one needs to read are as follows: 'Seminar on "The Purloined Letter" ', and 'Position of the Unconscious' (both in *Écrits: The First Complete Edition in English*), and 'The Neurotic Individual's Myth' (*Psychoanalytic Quarterly* 48, pp. 405–25).

Bettelheim: Deleuze and Guattari draw directly on Bettelheim's case analysis of 'Joey' in his *The Empty Fortress* in their account of desiring-machines. This text is additionally interesting for the fact that Bettelheim supplies pictures of Joey's machines.

Klein: Deleuze and Guattari range widely over Klein's works, but focus particularly on her case analysis of the ten-year-old boy Richard (aka 'Little Richard' or 'Dick') in their account of desiring-machines. Published as a book-length work, *Narrative of a Child Analysis*, this work is certainly worth dipping into, particularly the first few chapters which detail the establishment phase of the analysis. As with the Bettelheim book, it is the illustrations, in this case drawings by Richard himself, that prove the most illuminating. They show very clearly the extent to which it was the 'war' rather than his parents that caused his mental disturbance.

Reich: The importance of Reich to Deleuze and Guattari is obvious inasmuch that they frequently commend him for raising questions neglected by other psychoanalysts, but ultimately at the level of actual methodology they draw very little from his work. But having said that, it is certainly instructive to browse both *The Function of the Orgasm* and *The Mass Psychology of Fascism*. Reich's work is an early example of an attempt, albeit flawed, to apply psychoanalysis to contemporary political problems.

Historical materialism
Marx: Deleuze and Guattari are clearly committed to a Marxist view of the world, but their approach to Marx's work is by no means doctrinal. Marx isn't a writer that one can easily segment into key essays, so it is difficult to identify a useful specimen of his work that could serve as an introduction. But readers may find it useful to begin by reading the introduction to *Grundrisse* and the section on the general formula for capital in *Capital: Volume 1*. Also useful is the discussion of the tendency towards a falling rate of profit in *Capital: Volume 3*.

Nietzsche: Deleuze and Guattari profit a great deal from Nietzsche's *The Genealogy of Morals*, particularly the second essay on guilt, bad conscience and debt. This highly stimulating essay is relatively easy read by Nietzsche's standards and well worth the effort.

Foucault: At the end of chapter one, Deleuze and Guattari explicitly situate their work as a continuation of Foucault's critique of psychoanalysis in *Madness and Civilisation*. In particular one should read the chapter entitled 'The Birth of the Asylum'.

Sartre: Both Deleuze and Guattari have expressed a debt to Sartre. In *Anti-Oedipus* this debt is quite explicit – their discussion of molar and molecular owes a great deal to Sartre's analysis of groups in *Critique of Dialectical Reason: Volume 1* (see book 2, sections 1 and 2).

Fanon: *The Wretched of the Earth* is a key work for Deleuze and Guattari because in spite of its Freudian inspiration it demonstrates very clearly that delirium is racial and political before it is familial.

Turner: Deleuze and Guattari suggest that Victor Turner's famous essay on the practice of a Ndembu Doctor (chapter 10 of *The Forest of Symbols*) is a perfect example of schizoanalysis. For this reason alone it should be regarded as essential reading.

Literature
Artaud: It is well known that Deleuze and Guattari adopt Artaud's term 'body without organs' as their own. But what is less clear is how much their concept owes to Artaud. My feeling is that the connection between Artaud and Deleuze and Guattari should be treated carefully, as a source of inspiration perhaps rather than the original source of particular concepts. The following pieces, sampled in *Antonin Artaud: Selected Writings*, edited by Susan Sontag, are good for openers: 'The Nerve Meter', 'Voyage to the Land of Tarahumara', 'Van Gogh, the Man Suicided by Society', and perhaps most importantly of all, 'To Have Done with the Judgement of God'.

Lawrence: It would be difficult to overstate the importance of D.H. Lawrence's work, especially his later essays, to Deleuze and Guattari. In this regard, it is well worth reading the twin volumes *Psychoanalysis and the Unconscious* and *Fantasia of the Unconscious*. It should be borne in mind, however, that these are mythopoeic not philosophic works, so they need to be read with caution. While Deleuze and Guattari are sympathetic to their polemic spirit, they don't embrace their conceptual constructions.

Proust: It would be impossible to overstate the importance of Proust to Deleuze. Proust is a constant presence in all his work. And though it is a big ask to plough through all 3,000 pages of *Remembrance of Things Past*, it is certainly worth the effort to read at least the first volume *Swann's Way*.

Beckett: Although a difficult author, Beckett's great trilogy *Molloy, Malone Dies* and *The Unnameable*, is a crucial point of reference for Deleuze and Guattari's understanding of schizophrenia as a creative process and not just a destructive illness.

Büchner: Deleuze and Guattari make extensive use of Büchner's short piece *Lenz* (which is included in Penguin's edition of Büchner's *Complete Plays, Lenz and Other Writings*) in the discussion of desiring-machines. It is a beautiful piece of writing which imaginatively reconstructs a schizophrenic delirium.

Nerval: Nerval's 'Sylvie' (readily available in the Penguin edition of Nerval's *Selected Writings*) is a short and beautiful piece that, like *Lenz*, informs Deleuze and Guattari's discussion of the schizophrenic process.

Butler: Deleuze and Guattari identify Samuel Butler's 'Book of Machines' (chapter 23 of *Erewhon*) as the inspiration for their 'machinic vitalism'. It illuminates very usefully Deleuze and Guattari's twin notions of the non-totalized whole and part of no part.

BIBLIOGRAPHY

BY DELEUZE AND GUATTARI

Deleuze, G. and Guattari, F. (2004a) [new edition] *Anti-Oedipus*, trans R. Hurley, M. Seem and H. R. Lane, London and New York: Continuum.

Deleuze, G. and Guattari, F. (2002) [nouvelle édition augmentée] *L'Anti-Oedipe: Capitalisme et Schizophrénie*, Paris: Éditions de Minuit.

Deleuze, G. and Guattari, F. (2004b) [new edition] *A Thousand Plateaus*, trans Brian Massumi, London and New York: Continuum.

Deleuze, G. and Guattari, F. (2001) *Mille Plateaux: Capitalisme et Schizophrénie 2*, Paris: Éditions de Minuit.

Deleuze, G. and Guattari, F. (1994) *What is Philosophy?*, trans Hugh Tomlinson and Graham Burchell, New York: Columbia University Press.

Deleuze, G. and Guattari, F. (1991) *Qu'est-ce que la philosophie?*, Paris: Éditions de Minuit.

BY DELEUZE

Deleuze, G. (2006) *Two Regimes of Madness: Texts and Interviews 1975–1995*, edited by D. Lapoujade and trans A. Hodges and M. Taormina, New York: Semiotext(e).

Deleuze, G. (2003) *Deux Régimes de Fous: Textes et Entretiens 1975–1995*, Paris: Éditions de Minuit.

Deleuze, G. (2005a) *Cinema 1: The Movement-Image*, trans Hugh Tomlinson and Robert Galeta, London: Continuum.

Deleuze, G. (1983) *Cinéma 1: L'image-mouvement*, Paris: Éditions de Minuit.

Deleuze, G. (2005b) *Cinema 2: The Time-Image*, trans Hugh Tomlinson and Robert Galeta, London: Continuum.

Deleuze, G. (1985) *Cinéma 2: L'image-temps*, Paris: Éditions de Minuit.

Deleuze, G. (2004) *Desert Islands and Other Texts 1953–1974*, edited by David Lapoujade and trans M. Taormina, New York: Semiotext(e).

Deleuze, G. (2002) *L'île Déserte et Autres Textes: Textes et Entretiens 1953–1974*, Paris: Éditions de Minuit.

Deleuze, G. and Parnet, C. (2002) *Dialogues II*, trans H. Tomlinson and B. Habberjam, London: Continuum.

Deleuze, G. and Parnet, C. (1996) *Dialogues*, Paris: Flammarion.

Deleuze, G. (2000) *Proust and Signs: The Complete Text*, trans R. Howard, Minneapolis: University of Minnesota Press.

Deleuze, G. (1997) *Essays Critical and Clinical*, trans Daniel W. Smith and Michael A. Greco, Minneapolis: University of Minnesota Press.

Deleuze, G. (1995) *Negotiations*, trans Martin Joughin, New York: Columbia University Press.

Deleuze, G. (2003) *Pourparlers 1972–1990*, Paris: Éditions de Minuit.

Deleuze, G. (1994) *Difference and Repetition*, trans P. Patton, London: Athlone.

Deleuze, G. (2005) *Différence et repetition*, Paris: Presses Universitaires de France.

Deleuze, G. (1991) *Empiricism and Subjectivity: An Essay on Hume's Theory of Human Nature*, trans Constantin Boundas, New York: Columbia University Press.

Deleuze, G. (1998) [sixth edition] *Empirisme et Subjectivité: Essai sur la Nature Humaine selon Hume*, Paris: Presses Universitaires de France.

Deleuze, G. (1988) *Bergsonism*, trans H. Tomlinson and B. Habberjam, New York: Zone Books.

Deleuze, G. (1983) *Nietzsche and Philosophy*, trans Hugh Tomlinson, London: Athlone.

Deleuze, G. (2003) [fourth edition] *Nietzsche et la philosophie*, Paris: Presses Universitaires de France.

BY GUATTARI

Guattari, F. (2006) *The Anti-Oedipus Papers*, edited by S. Nadaud, trans K. Gotman, New York: Semiotext(e).

Guattari, F. (2004) *Écrits pour L'Anti-Oedipe*, edited by Stéphane Nadaud, Paris: Lignes-Manifeste.

Guattari, F. (1995a) *Chaosmosis: An Ethico-Aesthetic Paradigm*, trans P. Bains and J. Pefanis, Sydney: Power Publications.

Guattari, F. (1995b) *Chaosophy*, edited by S. Lotringer, New York: Semiotext(e).

ABOUT DELEUZE AND GUATTARI

Agamben, G. (1999) *Potentialities: Collected Essays in Philosophy*, edited by and trans D. Heller-Roazen, Stanford: Stanford University Press.

Alliez, É. (2006) '*Anti-Oedipus* – Thirty Years On (Between Art and Politics)', in M. Fuglsang and B.M. Sørensen, *Deleuze and The Social*, Edinburgh: Edinburgh University Press, pp. 135–68.

Ansell-Pearson, K. (1999) *Germinal Life: The Difference and Repetition of Deleuze*, London: Routledge.

Badiou, A. (2000) *Deleuze: The Clamour of Being*, trans L. Burchill, Minneapolis: University of Minnesota Press.

Balke, F. (1996) 'Sur la non-réception de Gilles Deleuze en Allemagne', trans J. Lacoste, *La Quinzaine Littéraire*, December-February, pp. 23–4.

Berressem, H. (2005) 'Is it Possible Not to Love Žižek? On Slavoj Žižek's Missed Encounter with Deleuze', *Electronic Book Review*.

Bogue, R. (1989) *Deleuze and Guattari*, London: Routledge.

Bonta, M. and Protevi, J. (2004) *Deleuze and Geophilosophy: A Guide and Glossary*, Edinburgh: Edinburgh University Press.

Buchanan, I. (2006a) 'Deleuze's "Life" Sentences', *Polygraph* 18, pp. 129–47.

Buchanan, I. (2006b) 'Is a Schizoanalysis of Cinema Possible?', *Revue CiNéMAS*, 16:2–3, pp. 117–45.

Buchanan, I. (2006c) 'Treatise on Militarism', in Buchanan and Parr (eds), *Deleuze and the Contemporary World*, Edinburgh: Edinburgh University Press, pp. 21–41.

Buchanan, I. (2006d) 'Practical Deleuzism and Postmodern Space', in Fuglsang and Sørensen (eds), *Deleuze and The Social*, Edinburgh: Edinburgh University Press, pp. 135–50.

Buchanan, I. and Parr, A. (2006) 'Introduction', in Buchanan and Parr (eds), *Deleuze and the Contemporary World*, Edinburgh: Edinburgh University Press, pp. 1–20.

Buchanan, I. (2000) *Deleuzism: A Metacommentary*, Edinburgh: Edinburgh University Press.

Colebrook, C. (2000) 'Is Sexual Difference a Problem?', in I. Buchanan and C. Colebrook (eds), *Deleuze and Feminist Theory*, Edinburgh: Edinburgh University Press, 110–27.

David-Ménard, M. (2005) *Deleuze et la psychanalyse*, Paris: Presses Universitaires de France.

Descombes, V. (1980) *Modern French Philosophy*, trans L. Scott-Fox and J. M. Harding, Cambridge: Cambridge University Press.

Faulkner, K. (2006) *Deleuze and the Three Syntheses of Time*, New York: Peter Lang.

Foss, P. and Morris, M. (1978) *Language, Sexuality and Subversion*, Sydney: Feral Publications.

Foucault, M. (1977) 'Intellectuals and Power', in D.F. Bouchard (ed), *Language, Counter-Memory and Practice: Selected Essays and Interviews by Michel Foucault*, Ithaca: Cornell University Press, pp. 205–17.

Foucault, M. (1975) *Discipline and Punish: The Birth of the Prison*, trans A. Sheridan, London: Penguin.

Frank, M. (1989) *What is Neostructuralism?*, trans S. Wilke and R. Gray, Minneapolis: University of Minnesota Press.

Genosko, G. (2007) 'The Figure of the Arab in *Three Billion Perverts*', *Deleuze Studies*, 1:1, pp. 60–78.

Genosko, G. (2002) *Félix Guattari: An Aberrant Introduction*, London: Continuum.

Hallward, P. (2006) *Out of this World: Deleuze and the Philosophy of Creation*, London: Verso.

Hardt, M. (1993) *Gilles Deleuze: An Apprenticeship in Philosophy*, Minneapolis: University of Minnesota Press.

Holland, E. (1999) *Deleuze and Guattari's Anti-Oedipus: Introduction to Schizoanalysis*, London: Routledge.

Jameson, F. (1999) 'Marxism and Dualism in Deleuze', in I. Buchanan (ed), *A Deleuzian Century?*, Durham, N.C.: Duke University Press, pp. 13–36.

Kerslake, C. (2007) *Deleuze and the Unconscious*, London: Continuum.

Lambert, G. (2006) *Who's Afraid of Deleuze and Guattari?*, London: Continuum.

Lotringer, S. (2001) 'Doing Theory', in S. Lotringer and S. Cohen (eds), *French Theory in America*, New York: Routledge, pp. 125–62.

Massumi, B. (1992) *A User's Guide to Capitalism and Schizophrenia: Deviations from Deleuze and Guattari*, Cambridge, Mass.: MIT Press.

May, T. (2005) *Gilles Deleuze: An Introduction*, Cambridge: Cambridge University Press.

Nadaud, S. (2006) 'Love Story between an Orchid and a Wasp', in Guattari, F. (2006), *The Anti-Oedipus Papers*, edited by S. Nadaud, trans K. Gotman, New York: Semiotext(e), pp. 11–22.

Parr, A. (ed) (2005) *The Deleuze Dictionary*, Edinburgh: Edinburgh University Press.

Patton, P. (1988) 'Marxism and Beyond: Strategies of Reterritoralisation', in C. Nelson and L. Grossberg (eds), *Marxism and the Interpretation of Culture*, London: Macmillan, pp. 123–39.

Smith, D. (2004) 'The Inverse Side of the Structure: Žižek on Deleuze and Lacan', *Criticism*, 46: 4, pp. 635–50.

Stivale, C. (ed) (2005) *Gilles Deleuze: Key Concepts*, Chesham: Acumen Publishing.

Thoburn, N. (2003) *Deleuze, Marx and Politics*, London: Routledge.

Williams, J. (2003) *Gilles Deleuze's Difference and Repetition: A Critical Introduction and Guide*, Edinburgh: Edinburgh University Press.

Žižek, S. (2005) 'Concesso non Dato', in G. Boucher *et al.* (eds), *Traversing the Fantasy: Critical Responses to Slavoj Žižek*, London: Ashgate, pp. 219–55.

Žižek, S. (2004a) *Organs without Bodies: On Deleuze and Consequences*, London: Routledge.

Žižek, S. (2004b) 'Notes on a Debate "From within the People"', *Criticism*, 46:4, pp. 661–6.

OTHER AUTHORS

Althusser, L. (1971) *Lenin and Philosophy*, trans B. Brewster, NY: Monthly Review Press.

Anderson, P. (1983) *In the Tracks of Historical Materialism*, London: Verso.

Arrighi, G. (1994) *The Long Twentieth Century: Money, Power, and the Origins of Our Times*, London: Verso.

Badiou, A. (2005) *Metapolitics*, trans J. Barker, London: Verso.

Badiou, A. (2001) *Ethics: An Essay on the Understanding of Evil*, trans P. Hallward, London: Verso.

Baudrillard, J. (1987) *Forget Foucault*, trans N. Dufresne, New York: Semiotext(e).

Benjamin, W. (1979) *One-Way Street*, trans E. Jephcott and K. Shorter, London: Verso.

Bettelheim, B. (1967) *The Empty Fortress: Infantile Autism and the Birth of the Self*, New York: Free Press.

Brink, A. (2000) *The Rights of Desire*, London: Vintage.

Buchanan, I. (2006d) *Fredric Jameson: Live Theory*, London: Continuum.

Büchner, G. (1993) [c. 1835] Lenz in *Büchner: Complete Plays, Lenz and Other Writings*, trans J. Reddick, London: Penguin, pp. 141–64.

Callinicos, A. (1989) *Against Postmodernism: A Marxist Critique*, Cambridge: Polity.

Callinicos, A. (1982) *Is there a Future for Marxism?*, London: Macmillan.

Certeau, M. de (1997) *The Capture of Speech and Other Political Writings*, trans T. Conley, Minneapolis: University of Minnesota Press.

Certeau, M. de (1984) *The Practice of Everyday Life*, trans S. Rendall, Berkeley: University of California Press.

Cockburn, P. (2006) *The Occupation: War and Resistance in Iraq*, London: Verso.

Conrad, J. (2000) [1900] *Lord Jim*, London: Penguin.

Davis, M. (2006) *Planet of Slums*, London: Verso.

De Landa, M. (2006) *A New Philosophy of Society: Assemblage Theory and Social Complexity*, London: Continuum.

Dews, P. (1987) *Logics of Disintegration: Post-structuralist Thought and the Claims of Critical Theory*, London: Verso.

Dine, P. (1994) *Images of the Algerian War: French Fiction and Film, 1954–1992*, Oxford: Clarendon Press.

Fields, B. (1984) 'French Maoism', in S. Sayres *et al.* (eds), *The 60s without Apology*, Minneapolis: University of Minnesota Press, pp. 148–77.

Fitrakis, R.J., Rosenfeld, S. and Wasserman, H. (2006) *What Happened in Ohio? A Documentary Record of Theft and Fraud in the 2004 Election*, New York: New Press.

Frank, T. (2004) *What's the Matter with Kansas? How Conservatives Won the Heart of America*, New York: Metropolitan Books.

Frank, T. (1997) *The Conquest of Cool: Business Culture, Counterculture, and the Rise of Hip Consumerism*, Chicago: Chicago University Press.

Freud, S. (1991) [1923] 'The Ego and the Id', in A. Richards (ed), *On Metapsychology: Penguin Freud Library Volume 11*, trans J. Strachey, London: Penguin, pp. 350–401.

Freud, S. (1990) *Case Histories II: Penguin Freud Library Volume 9*, trans J. Strachey, London: Penguin.

Freud, S. (1979) [1911] 'Psychoanalytic Notes on an Autobiographical Account of a Case of Paranoia (Dementia Paranoides)', in A. Richards (ed), *Case Histories II: Penguin Freud Library Volume 9*, trans J. Strachey, London: Penguin, pp. 141–223.

Freud, S. (1976) [1900] *The Interpretation of Dreams: Penguin Freud Library Volume 4*, London: Penguin.

George, S. (2004) *Another World is Possible If . . .*, London: Verso.

Hardt, M. and Negri, A. (2000) *Empire*, Cambridge, Mass.: Harvard University Press.

Holloway, J. (2005) [new edition] *Change the World Without Taking Power*, London: Pluto Press.

Irigaray, L. (1985) *This Sex which is not One*, trans C. Porter, Ithaca: Cornell University Press.

Jameson, F. (2006) 'Live Jameson', in I. Buchanan, *Frederick Jameson: Live Theory*, London: Continuum, pp. 120–32.

Jameson, F. (2005) *Archaeologies of the Future: The Desire Called Utopia and Other Science Fictions*, London: Verso.

Jameson, F. (1994) *The Seeds of Time*, New York: Columbia.

Jameson, F. (1991) *Postmodernism, or, The Cultural Logic of Late Capitalism*, London: Verso.

Jameson, F. (1990) *Late Marxism: Adorno, or, The Persistence of the Dialectic*, London: Verso.

Jameson, F. (1988a) *The Ideologies of Theory: Essays 1971–1986. Volume 1: Situations of Theory*, Minneapolis: University of Minnesota Press.

Jameson, F. (1988b) *The Ideologies of Theory: Essays 1971–1986. Volume 2: Syntax of History*, Minneapolis: University of Minnesota Press.

Jameson, F. (1972) *The Prison-House of Language: A Critical Account of Structuralism and Russian Formalism*, Princeton: Princeton University Press.

Jameson, F. (1971) *Marxism and Form: Twentieth-Century Dialectical Theories of Literature*, Princeton: Princeton University Press.

Jardine, A. (1985) *Gynesis: Configurations of Woman and Modernity*, Ithaca: Cornell University Press.

Klein, N. (2007) 'Sacrificial Wolfie', *The Nation*, 14 May, p. 10.

Klein, N. (2001) 'Reclaiming the Commons', *New Left Review*, 9, pp. 81–9.

Klein, N. (2000) *No Logo*, London: Flamingo.

Lacan, J. (2006) *Écrits: The First Complete Edition in English*, trans B. Fink, New York and London: W.W. Norton.

Laclau, E. and Mouffe, C. (1985) *Hegemony and Socialist Strategy: Towards a Radical Democratic Politics*, London: Verso.

Laing, R.D. (1990) [1959] *The Divided Self: An Existential Study in Sanity and Madness*, London: Penguin.

Marx, K. (1976) [1867] *Capital: A Critique of Political Economy Volume 1*, trans B. Fowkes, London: Penguin.

Marx, K. (1973) [c. 1857–8] *Grundrisse: Foundations of the Critique of Political Economy*, trans M. Nicolaus, London: Penguin.

Negri, A. (2004) *Negri on Negri: Antonio Negri in Conversation with Anne Dufourmantelle*, trans M.B. DeBevoise, London: Routledge.

Oury, J. (2007) 'The Hospital is Ill: An Interview with Jean Oury', trans D. Reggio, *Radical Philosophy*, 143, pp. 32–45.

Parenti, M. (1995) *Against Empire*, San Francisco: City Lights Books.

Proust, M. (2000) *Swann's Way*, trans C.K. Moncrief, London: Penguin Classics.

Rancière, J. (1999) *Disagreement: Politics and Philosophy*, trans J. Rose, Minneapolis: University of Minnesota Press.

Retort (2005) *Afflicted Powers: Capital and Spectacle in a New Age of War*, London: Verso.

Ross, K. (2002) *May '68 and its Afterlives*, Chicago: Chicago University Press.

Sartre, J.-P. (2004) *Critique of Dialectical Reason: Volume One*, trans A. Sheridan-Smith, London: Verso.
Schreber, D. (2000) *Memoirs of my Nervous Illness*, trans I. Macalpine and R. Hunter, New York: New York Review of Books.
Sloterdijk, P. (1987) *Critique of Cynical Reason*, trans M. Eldred, Minneapolis: University of Minnesota Press.
Theweleit, K. (1987) *Male Fantasies* (2 volumes), trans S. Conway with E. Carter and C. Turner, Minneapolis: University of Minnesota Press.
Tournier, M. (1988) *The Wind Spirit: An Autobiography*, trans A. Goldhammer, Boston: Beacon Press.
Wolin, R. (2007) 'Veiled Intolerance', *The Nation*, 9 April, pp. 25–30.
Žižek, S. (2006) *The Parallax View*, Cambridge, Mass.: MIT Press.
Žižek, S. (2002) [second edition] *For They Know not what they do: Enjoyment as a Political Factor*, London: Verso.
Žižek, S. (2001) [second edition] *Enjoy Your Symptom! Jacques Lacan in Hollywood and Out*, London: Routledge.
Žižek, S. (1993) *Tarrying with the Negative: Kant, Hegel, and the Critique of Ideology*, Durham: Duke University Press.
Žižek, S. (1991) *Looking Awry: An Introduction to Jacques Lacan Through Popular Culture*, Cambridge, Mass.: MIT Press.
Žižek, S. (1989) *The Sublime Object of Ideology*, London: Verso.

INDEX

CPSIA information can be obtained at www.ICGtesting.com
Printed in the USA
LVOW10s1105300716

498418LV00016B/249/P